THE SEVEN

7

FIGURE OUT
FIND OUT
SCOPE OUT
WRITE OUT
CARRY OUT
MEASURE OUT
SHOUT OUT

OUTS

THE SEVEN

7

FIGURE **OUT**
FIND **OUT**
SCOPE **OUT**
WRITE **OUT**
CARRY **OUT**
MEASURE **OUT**
SHOUT **OUT**

OUTS

**STRATEGIC
PLANNING
MADE EASY
FOR CHARTER
SCHOOLS**

BRIAN L. CARPENTER, PhD

FOREWORD BY JAMES N. GOENNER

NATIONAL CHARTER SCHOOLS INSTITUTE
Mt. Pleasant, Michigan

Published by The National Charter Schools Institute
Mt. Pleasant, Michigan

Publisher's Cataloging-in-Publication Data
Carpenter, Brian L.

 The seven outs : strategic planning made easy for charter schools / Brian L. Carpenter.—Mt. Pleasant, Mich.: The National Charter Schools Institute, 2008.

   p. ; cm.

   ISBN13: 978-0-9788573-2-5

   1. Charter schools—Administration—United States.
   2. School management and organization—United States.
   I. Title.

LB2806.36 C37 2008
371.01-dc22   2008925959

Project coordination by Jenkins Group, Inc
Interior layout design by Brooke Camfield
www.BookPublishing.com

Printed in the United States of America

In Memory of
Joseph P. Overton, III (1960–2003)

A deeply missed friend, visionary, and indomitable
school choice advocate.

As the former Senior Vice President of
The Mackinac Center for Public Policy,

Joe continuously urged those of us who reported
to him to "Focus like a laser."

I pass his exhortation to you.

Contents

Illustrations

Foreword

As a former baseball player, I never got excited about being *out*. So you can imagine the thoughts that raced through my mind when Brian offered me the opportunity to write the preface for his new book on strategic planning called the *Seven Outs*. I think I even went as far as making a wisecrack something like, "Seven outs is more than two innings worth."

But as a good coach would do, Brian explained to me that the purpose of the *Seven Outs* is to provide a team—in this case a school—with a framework for helping its students reach their full potential and avoid being called out and no longer being allowed to play the game by the umpire—in this case the school's authorizer.

As the leader of the nation's largest university authorizer of charter public schools, I see promising evidence everyday of how the charter strategy is acting as a catalyst to transform public education by infusing the powerful dynamics of choice, change, and competition—and bringing *real* accountability to the "system." Old assumptions are being questioned, results are being examined and made transparent, expectations are being raised, and the standard excuses are no longer being tolerated. These are good things.

With the promise of the charter strategy in motion, focus is rightly shifting to how well the schools being established via a charter contract are performing. It is important to understand that charter schools are as diverse as the students they serve. So while the promise of the charter strategy is working, there is no guarantee that every charter school will produce outstanding results.

This brings me to why I am so excited to commend this book to you. You see, I still have some competitive juices flowing through my veins. And while some view charter public schools as an experiment, I view America as the real experiment. The idea of a free people coming together to form a more perfect union that gives all people the same opportunity for life, liberty, and the pursuit of happiness is still a relatively new idea in the course of human history.

Moreover, each day we hear how global competition is challenging America's economic prowess and that we are moving at breakneck speed to a technology driven, knowledge-based economy.

If we are to compete effectively in this global marketplace, it is imperative that we better prepare students. This thinking is not new. In 1983, the landmark report, *A Nation At Risk,* warned that "the educational foundations of our society are presently being eroded by a rising tide of mediocrity that threatens our very future as a Nation and a people. What was unimaginable a generation ago has begun to occur—others are matching and surpassing our educational attainments."

So you see much is riding on the charter strategy and the schools established via a charter. Many of the people that have stepped up to advocate and implement the strategy along with those who have founded schools have given blood, sweat and tears. That said, the start-up days are over and expectations are being raised.

Getting a charter school up and running is not sufficient. Charter schools must consistently produce great results for students and taxpayers. While nearly everyone agrees with this notion, not all schools know how to get there.

This is where the *Seven Outs* comes into play. As *Good to Great* author Jim Collins writes, "Greatness is not a function of circumstance. Greatness . . . is largely a matter of conscious choice, and discipline." So if your school is ready to make the conscious decision to pursue greatness, the *Seven Outs* will provide you with the roadmap for getting there.

I hope your team hits it out of the park for the kids!

Regards,

James N. Goenner
Executive Director

The Center for Charter Schools
Central Michigan University

Acknowledgments

One of the fun things about writing a book is that you get a rare opportunity to acknowledge for the record, how blessed you are by colleagues who enrich your professional life. As the length of the list that follows attests, I have more than my fair share of friends, inspiring colleagues, and clients to whom I owe a debt of gratitude. If the reader will indulge me, I'd like to thank a few of them.

First, although this book is primarily about strategic planning rather than governance, I'd like to express my appreciation to Dr. John Carver for creating Policy Governance. Some thirty years after he conceived it, Policy Governance continues to be the only comprehensive framework for governance in existence. John and his wife, Miriam, have, as a result of their extensive writing and teaching, influenced and inspired many—including me—to fervently advance the concepts of good governance.

Although I've directly referenced the Carvers no less than 19 times throughout this book, their names could probably have legitimately appeared on nearly every page, because their thinking on governance informs much of what I think defines the proper role of the board in strategic planning. In so acknowledging this, however, I want readers to be clear that this is not a book that explains Policy Governance. Nor can a board that utilizes *The Seven Outs* claim to be using Policy Governance, although the latter influenced the development of the former. If your board wants to implement Policy Governance—something any board would be well-advised to consider—you should begin by reading John's phenomenal book, *Boards That Make a Difference.*

Another friend and colleague that challenges my thinking is Jim Goenner, a man whose ideas about, and commitment to, charter schools are nationally felt. Jim is the executive director of The Center for Charter Schools at Central Michigan University, the largest university authorizer in the country (with 58 schools in its portfolio, and counting). Because the National Charter Schools Institute is also affiliated with CMU, I have the good fortune of having an office in the same building as Jim. From this close proximity, I've had the chance to regularly interact with him during the past three years. He is an exceptional thinker and a brilliant strategist. We exchange ideas so often that I sometimes can't remember where his ideas stop and mine start. But I can say for sure, that a presentation Jim gave about a year ago was the genesis for the section in this book dealing with school measurement.

Jim has also surrounded himself with a dream team, several of whom have been a force for good in my life as we have collaborated on projects in the past few years. The team is big, so space limits me to naming those few with whom I've worked most closely on occasion. Among these, Cindy Schumacher heads the list for her tireless contributions in helping the two organizations waltz together. Angie Irwin, Mark Weinberg, Dr. Harry Ross, Mary Kay Shields, and Tim Odykirk are also esteemed colleagues. Next, there are my senior management colleagues at the Institute: Amy Van Atten, Penny Davis, Ed Roth, and Rich Scherf. Each possesses a unique genius and is fun to work with. They expect nothing less than my best and they reciprocate by giving the same, as do all of our associate consultants and support staff members. They are all—to borrow high praise reserved for top-performing Marines—*hard chargers*. I commend them for being "20 percenters"—a compliment whose meaning will be clear when you've finished this book.

I also want to thank someone with whom I have only corresponded through email, but his books have transformed not only the way I think about organizational effectiveness, but also the way I approach every area of my life. Richard Koch is an international bestselling author from Great Britain who has written more on the 80/20 principle than anyone. I am compelled to personally thank him for explaining an observation made by an Italian economist in such a way that no client or project of mine now escapes its benefits.

My hat is off again to Dave Bardallis who edited this book (in addition to my previous one). I wish he could be with me to take a bow in all the instances where people have complimented the way I write. They never know, but I do, how much they're complimenting the caliber of Dave's work. If readers think this book is about the right length, they should send Dave a thank you note for excising over 1,000 words from the original manuscript as skillfully as a surgeon removes a tumor.

Lastly, I appreciate the many clients and colleagues across the country that have welcomed me into their schools and associations. There are too many of you to name here, but I trust that each of you knows that your work on behalf of children inspires me to continue writing—as well as eating in airports, waiting interminably at baggage carousels, and sleeping in hotels where complimentary breakfasts consist of simple sugars and other empty carbohydrates. Such things really are minor inconveniences compared to being graced with the privilege of serving you.

Introduction

Except perhaps for global warming, healing your inner child, and achieving financial success in life, I doubt that few topics have been as exhaustively written about as organizational strategic planning. Curious to know just how many books on the topic are actually out there, I pointed my browser to Amazon.com as I started writing, guessing I would find 750 to 2,000. Not even close.

At that time, Amazon listed 41,226 titles. Yes, you read that right, and no, 41,226 is not a typo. In order to convert this to a number that conveys a meaning we can understand, I decided to break it down into how long it would take to read these at the rate of one per week. The answer? If you read one book every week, it would take you slightly longer than 15 years to read them all. This is sufficiently long enough to give pause before writing a new book, even to consultants who, as a matter of routine, assume that their stuff is good enough to compete.

And if the number alone isn't daunting enough, you have to figure that there can't really be much new to say on a topic about which trillions of words have already been published.

But I proceeded to write anyway. Why? Well, I *am* a consultant, but besides that, I have four primary reasons.

1. You Asked For It

I wrote this book because you asked for it. Well, maybe not *you*, specifically. But you, generally, as in all of you who lead charter schools or have
participated in conferences with whom I've had the pleasure of more than
two minutes' interaction over the past few years. It's not hyperbole to say
that if there has been a single recurring question that people keep asking
me, it is, "Can you help our board with strategic planning?"

So, to all who have asked or who are asking by reading this book,
my answer is, *yes*. (Thanks for asking, too, because your questions help
me better recognize those issues most important to you and the charter
schools you govern or manage.)

2. If You're Going to Buy a New Suit, Why Not Get One That Fits?

Charter school leaders need resources that are tailored to their unique
challenges. However, to the best of my knowledge, despite the fact that
there are tons of books on strategic planning, *there are no books that
specifically address strategic planning for charter schools*. The diligent
inquirer is left to his or her own devices to sort through a dump-truck
load of books on strategic planning *for other sectors*, including businesses,
nonprofit organizations, and individuals. With a few mouse clicks, you
can even find a few strategic planning resources tailored for independent
schools (i.e., private schools that are tuition-funded rather than taxpayer-
funded). But there is nothing for charter schools.

Among the books in all these categories, some are exceptional, as
acknowledged in part by the references citing them throughout this book.
But as valuable as such books may be for *their intended audiences*, you
have to do a fair amount of retooling in order to apply their lessons to
charter schools. After all, your school is not in business to make money like
a for-profit organization—although you do have to *make money* to stay
in business. Your school may be a not-for-profit organization (as required
of charter schools in some states), but unlike most nonprofits, fundraising is not your primary staple—consumption of public tax dollars is.

Your charter makes you a public school but you're not a conventional public school. Among the key differences is the fact that no one assigns students and teachers to charter schools.

This key difference alone sets charters apart because they must compete in order to operate. This means your strategic plan has to include some *market-like considerations*, such as whether the geographical area from which you recruit your enrollment is projected to grow. And although private schools face the same challenges with respect to recruiting students, charter schools also have an unprecedented level of accountability to their authorizers or sponsors. Few private schools have any such similar layer of accountability.

If you have time to translate the strategic planning lessons from other sectors to your school, there is certainly value to be gained. For example, one of my favorite books on strategic planning is a business book, *Execution: The Discipline of Getting Things Done* by Ram Charan and Larry Bossidy. Perhaps more than any other single volume, this book helps inform my thinking about the core elements that must be considered in strategic planning. (I will mention their work several times in this book.) But the book cannot be applied wholesale to charter schools because its message is for-profit in nature. The retooling job, then, becomes what to leave in and what to take out, as well as, how to recast what's left so that it fits your charter school.

This retooling may be difficult, especially for board members or new executives who don't necessarily come to the table with school oversight or organizational strategic planning expertise. On top of which, if you're like most charter school board members and executive directors I have the privilege of knowing, you're already spread pretty thin with multiple commitments. One of my purposes, then, is to shorten your learning curve while simultaneously maximizing your understanding—by creating a resource specifically written for charters.

3. You Won't Remember Key Lessons If They're Dull

Many have observed that we tend to remember central ideas when they are part of a story. This truth is explained remarkably well in *Made to Stick: Why Some Ideas Survive and Others Die* by brothers Dan Heath and Chip Heath. The authors do a delightful job of unpacking the six elements that make some ideas "sticky," i.e., memorable. One of the six elements is that people remember stories.

So, when was the last time you read a strategic planning book that told a story? Never? Consequently, how well do you remember the central ideas of the book? Yeah, me neither.

In this book, I tell the story of BPCS, a fictional charter school whose initials stand for *Breezy Palms Charter School*. The events and characters in this book are made up, or sufficiently re-engineered as to make identifying them with any individual or school impossible. In other words, if there are similarities between your school and the BPCS story, it's purely by chance. With that said, there will be similarities, because most charter schools face the same kinds of challenges.

But back to my point on being memorable. If the Heaths and others are right—and I think they are—you're more likely to remember key strategic planning ideas because this book tells a story.

4. You Need to Know What to Do First, Second, Third, etc.

The ultimate emphasis of this book is on what to *do* and in what order to do it. Asking and answering the right questions early in the strategic planning process, for example, will strongly influence how well your plan is executed and how well your board can assess the performance of the school. When your board members and executive[1] finish reading this book, they should know exactly where to begin the process, how

---

1   Throughout this book, I interchangeably use the titles executive, CEO, administrator, principal, school leader, etc. to refer to the professional staff member who is in charge of the operations of the school. As I explain later in the book, I prefer the word executive because it rightly emphasizes the skill at which, above all others, that individual must be master.

to manage it along the way, and how to evaluate the school's progress against the plan. *Practical applications* are the watchwords.

This book does, however, incorporate some theory into its message. Note that my use of the word *theory* is in the scientific sense of the word, meaning a conceptual model or framework, which is different than *theory* in the vernacular sense (usually meaning a hunch or an intuition). But don't let your eyes glaze over as a result. As both a reader and a writer, I'm sensitive to the fact that books should be written for audiences, not for authors to impress themselves by waxing eloquently on academic topics. Speaking for myself, I'd rather eat unsalted Styrofoam than digest a dry theoretical treatise on strategic planning, so I wouldn't ask you to, either.

So why all this talk about theory? You might be thinking, "Do I really need to understand strategic planning theory?" The answer is yes—at least a little bit. Let me illustrate why.

Every time I board an airplane, my apprehension about crashing is somewhat mitigated by my confidence that the pilots, in addition to their practical training, *have a good understanding of the theory of flying*, (i.e., glide, lift, thrust, and so on). The theoretical stuff is drilled into them in training, and with good reason. As soon as they encounter a problem for which they've received no specific training, they have to combine *their knowledge of theory* with their experience to solve the problem. Take away the theory, and the only thing left is experience, which might not be sufficient to get the plane safely back on the ground in the event of an emergency.

As a charter school board member or executive, you're going to encounter situations that are not described in this book for the simple reason that I obviously can't possibly know the details of the specific challenges facing your school. In the absence of actual consulting, understanding and applying sound theory is the next best thing. (Of course, this book is not intended to replace the advice of legal counsel. The other usual standard disclaimers apply as well.)

So there you are. Four good reasons to make this book number 41,227 (or whatever the number is by the time this goes to press).

As always, I love to hear from my readers. You're welcome to contact me with your comments, questions, or suggestions for improvement. These are often the impetus for new writing ideas or services intended to build stronger, more effective charter schools that prepare kids to go where we cannot. You can contact me through the National Charter Schools Institute at www.NationalCharterSchools.org.

Now, let's get you going on strategic planning for your school.

Best regards,
Brian L. Carpenter, Ph.D.
CEO
National Charter Schools Institute
March 2008

PART One

The Breezy Palms Charter School Story

The Stage is Set

Imagine yourself sitting in a darkened auditorium where you are about to watch a play. As the drama unfolds, you will be able to observe the actions of seven board members and the executive director of the fictitious Breezy Palms Charter School, along with a few supporting characters. From your vantage point, you'll observe a couple of BPCS board meetings as though you're in the room with them, and you'll gain an insider's look at some of their thoughts and values.

As the narrator of this story, I will begin by telling you about Sally. She has just wheeled her car into the school parking lot at 6:17 p.m. It is early spring, and the sun is already down. The night sky only added to her feeling of fatigue after another ten-hour day at the insurance company where she manages a sales team. She sighs as she glances at the folder lying next to her. As she reaches for it, she looks at her watch, confirming what she already knows: She is late for the special meeting posted to start at six o'clock.

She swallows hard as she thinks about the letter in the folder. She doesn't want to acknowledge the existence of that letter to herself, much less discuss it *and* enter it into the board's minutes for the whole world to see. In her mind's eye, she can already imagine certain parents frantically calling one another, fanning the flames of a fire that already threatened to engulf the school.

It's just not fair, she thinks as she walks briskly toward the fourth-grade classroom where the board had been meeting at least monthly since the school opened nearly five years ago. During the first two years, they often met at least twice a month.

She knows they'd been fortunate to cobble together enough funding to acquire an old, unused elementary school building. The floor tiles are dingy from countless decades of waxing and buffing, but she thinks the hallways always have a cheerful feeling to them because of the colorful artwork that adorns the bulletin boards, courtesy of the kids at Breezy Palms Charter School. The age of the building, combined with the lack of funding for major improvements, sometimes prompts Sally to joke that the board is flying a jumbo jet held together with duct tape and rubber bands. Tonight, however, no one will be in the mood for jokes.

The curtain rises.

The Board Meeting No One Ever Imagined Having

"**H**ello, everyone," Sally said, entering the classroom. The school's executive, four of the seven board members, and about a dozen parents stood visiting one another. As they greeted her, she quickly responded, "Sorry I'm running late. Let's go ahead and get started."

As the members of the board took their places around the table, Sally's mind was on the parents. She couldn't recall seeing that many at a board meeting except the time when the board changed the lunch schedule a couple of years ago, eliminating ten minutes from recess. *This is just dandy*, she thought. *We can't get parents to volunteer or regularly come to board meetings, but they can make time for tonight?*

She felt a twinge of regret for accepting the board's nomination to become president a year earlier. The previous five years, counting the year they were preoperational, Sam chaired the board. He always seemed disorganized, but he was friendly and truth be told, no one else wanted the job. Last year, citing too many other commitments in his life, he abruptly resigned from the board. When the other board members enthusiastically nominated Sally, she reluctantly accepted.

"Okay," she said, "it's 6:21, and I see we have a quorum present. I hereby officially call this special meeting of the BPCS board to order."

5

Looking around the table, she added, "I got an email from Mark sending his regrets. He's in Houston on business." Though she didn't convey it in her tone, his absence irritated her because he often missed two or three meetings in a row, requiring the rest of the board to bring him up to speed when he returned. "And I haven't heard from Claudia." She glanced at Rebecca, the board secretary, who was already taking minutes.

"I'm going to cut right to the chase," continued Sally, unable to camouflage the anxiety in her voice, "I'm afraid I have some unfortunate news." The parents huddled quietly off to the side. The board members were rapt with attention. Although no one besides Sally had actually seen the letter, word through the grapevine was out and everyone anticipated the blow.

"As you know, last month BPCS was visited by an evaluation team from our authorizer. I admit that I don't fully understand what it is they do or how they do it. Actually, I don't think I've ever met any of them. But I guess part of their job is to weigh how we're doing as a school and to decide whether or not to renew our charter, which expires at the end of this school year—in about three months.

"We . . ." Sally, not normally at a loss for words, paused. "They said that they are not going to renew our charter. I received a letter yesterday from them by certified mail." She started to pick up the folder to pass the letter around to the board.

The parents immediately began talking to one another, causing Sally to have to call for order. "Okay, okay," she said. "I know this is not good news, but let's try to discuss this in an organized manner. We need to decide what to do." As she spoke, she changed her mind and laid the folder down, deciding that it would be better for everyone to speak their mind before they read the letter.

"What to do?" demanded Steve. "What do you mean, *what to do*? We fight them or sue them or whatever! I just don't understand this. We've worked so hard. And for what? To have those people"—sounding contemptuous of the authorizing evaluation team, which is how he intended it—"come around our school once a year and then tell us after five years they don't think we're good enough to be a school anymore? This is a bunch of bull, that's what!"

Steve's face grew redder as his words tumbled out faster. "Besides, they can't do that to us, can they? I don't see what gives them the authority. We've worked hard to get this place up and running. I've personally put in countless hours repainting the hallways and classrooms when we bought this building.

"Running a school takes a lot of work," he went on, sputtering. "There are a lot of people who put in many hours around here. What do they want from us? There's nothing wrong with our school. Have you ever been inside Oak Lawn Elementary? There's no way I'm sending my kids back to that gulag."

Sally winced at Steve's use of the word *gulag* because some of her clients worked there and because she didn't want an antagonistic relationship with other local public schools. She wished Steve would exhibit a more professional demeanor in board meetings, recalling many past instances of his ill temper, as he continued rambling.

"I just think this is a bunch of bull, that's what," he finished, before realizing he was repeating himself. "I don't think so!" he added lamely.

Sally thought he sounded more like a general opining on war strategy than a board member of a charter school. In fairness, Steve *had* worked hard. He would do anything. She remembered the time he and two other volunteers spent an entire Saturday spreading pea-gravel around the playground. On another occasion, though it had taken a substantial part of several board meetings to organize, Steve spearheaded a project to build bookshelves for every classroom. He even brought in his own power tools for others to use. The project ran so efficiently, some parent volunteers complimented Steve, saying that he ran the show like it was an assembly line. *High praise for a doer*, thought Sally.

Still perturbed, however, by the way he referred to Oak Lawn, Sally reminded herself that people were going to likely need to vent their frustrations tonight before a solution could be constructed. Her mind jumped ahead to how she should respond to parents when it came time for public comment. She recognized some of the faces in the room as well-practiced gossips, but she noticed one person she didn't know. He was scribbling notes on a reporter's pocket pad. *Wonderful*, she thought. *That's all we need now is for the newspaper to turn this into a media circus.* Breezy Palms had always felt like an unloved stepchild compared to the way the local paper reported favorably on the other public schools.

Paul, the new BPCS executive, sat frowning during Steve's rant. He was only half-listening as he contemplated the reality of the challenges the school had been facing. The students were not performing well on the state exams when he accepted the job a year earlier, but he felt that there was potential if the school had a little more time. Now he wondered whether he should update his résumé. After running schools for 12 years, he knew full well that executives have a small window each year in which to find another job, usually somewhere between March and June—and June is pushing it. Schools still recruiting a new director beyond summer often have "iceberg" governance problems—board dysfunctions that are not readily apparent in the interview. *And it's already April 8th*, he thought. *I sure didn't anticipate having to look for a new school in just one year.*

Paul's attention returned as another board member, J.J., began speaking.

"Well," J.J. said, choosing his words carefully, as usual, "this is certainly going to hit our families hard." The parents again mumbled to each other. Acknowledging their concerns, J.J. continued, "I know how hard this would be for my family if my children were still school age and we had to change schools."

It was precisely for his even-keeled temperament that Sally had asked J.J., one of her longtime insurance clients, to join the board about seven months after the school became operational. His smile and his eyes always reminded Sally of her own grandfather, and his easygoing demeanor naturally tended to put those around him at ease. As he paused, she recalled the times she told him that he would have made a great principal were he not a fifth-generation dairy farmer. He once replied that principals have a harder job, but unlike dairy farmers, at least they can get a vacation away from *their* clients.

"It seems to me," J.J. continued, "that we ought to consider putting together a committee to look at our options." A few parents nodded in agreement.

"But what can we *do*?" Steve retorted. "Those people just come in here like they own the place and tell us we can't be a school anymore. It's not fair! We need to *do* something."

J.J. just looked at Steve, pursed his lips, and nodded his head, as if to say he agreed and he understood Steve's frustration. To everyone's relief, this had the effect of causing Steve to relax. He sat back in his chair and exhaled, signaling, for the moment at least, he had worn himself out venting.

Deborah seized the opportunity the lull presented and asked to be recognized. "Did the authorizer say exactly what's wrong? I mean, is this a done deal or are there specific things we can address?" The others nodded.

"After all," she continued, "with accreditation visits, schools get a chance to rebut the findings if they disagree. I myself have participated in several visiting teams to other schools and I know for certain there is a process if the school disagrees with the team's findings."

No one immediately replied. As a high school teacher for more than twenty years in another area school, Deborah's experience was highly regarded by the board. Deborah avoided flaunting her position as an educator, but she knew—and so did the board—that she knew more about schools than the rest of the board members put together. Her addition to the board three years earlier gave everyone the feeling that they had recruited a pro to their minor league team.

Paul finally spoke, hesitantly, because as BPCS's third executive director in four years, he still felt like an outsider even though he knew that most of the board liked him. "I don't want to contradict your point about accreditation visiting teams, Deborah, but the board should note that this is a different situation. As a charter school, our charter is a kind of contract that basically says if we meet its terms, we can continue to operate as a public school. If we don't meet those terms—student performance in this case—then the authorizer can decline to renew the contract.

"Still, to your point on appealing the decision," he said, looking first at Deborah and then at the other board members, "we ought to give it a try. For one thing, we don't have anything to lose. Besides, to the best of my understanding, the authorizing staff's evaluation isn't technically *the* official decision. Not to diminish its importance, but my understanding is that it's a staff recommendation to their governing board. It's their board that actually makes the decision."

Paul had spoken tactfully, but Deborah was miffed that Paul knew more about charter schools than she did. Not wanting to be seen as insecure, however, she said only, "Yes, that's what I meant. We should appeal to their board."

The only board member present who hadn't spoken was Rebecca. No one thought much about this, however, because Rebecca was quiet by nature. When she did speak, it was usually so softly others had to strain to hear her. And even then, she probably never said more than three consecutive sentences in a board meeting—ever. Instead, as other board members expressed themselves, she sat diligently taking the minutes. The job of board secretary suited her. She liked details and she had a penchant for accuracy.

Now, as she recorded what people were saying, Sally looked directly at her. "Rebecca," she said, "I'm wondering what your thoughts are."

Rebecca looked up from her note-taking, caught off guard. Usually, the board didn't specifically seek her opinion and she was content to contribute to the board by being the official keeper of the board's records. "Well, I think we ought to see if we can establish a dialogue with whoever is in charge of the authorizing office and get *their* advice," she said. "I assume that they're only trying to do their job and that they don't see themselves as our adversary. Asking them what they think we should do might be a good first step."

Pleased that Rebecca had provided a positive segue toward a solution, Sally thanked everyone for their thoughts. She was about to open the meeting to public comment, when, true to form, Claudia burst into the room. It was now 7:13. *Almost an hour after we started*, thought Sally.

"Hi everyone," said Claudia breezily. "I know I'm a bit late, but I had to drop off the kids at the babysitter because Alex is out of town. What's up?" she said, catching Sally's solemn expression. "Is this about the new playground equipment we've been talking about ordering? If so, I have some new ideas about color schemes."

"Thanks for making it tonight," Sally said. "I'm afraid it's more serious than that. But rather than rehash the past hour, let me just say I have a letter from our authorizer informing us that our charter is not going to be renewed at the end of this school year. We are actually about to open the meeting to public comments. Since it's getting late and people have other commitments, we're going to have to fill you in on the details later."

"Uh, well, all right," Claudia said, her words drifting off in astonishment.

"Okay," said Sally, straightening. "I'd like to open this meeting to comments from the public. But first, I want to thank you all for coming out tonight. The board always appreciates it when people are interested enough in their school to show up at meetings." *Do you get it now, when it may be too late?* she mentally added.

"I know there are a lot of concerns, and this is a big challenge, but I'm going to ask each person to limit his or her comments to two minutes. This way, everyone can be heard and we can still get home at a decent hour. Also, as a matter of protocol, the board is not going to respond to any statements or questions tonight. We will, however, communicate any decisions within 24 hours. Who would like to go first?"

The general mood was one of anxiety. Not all of the parents spoke, but many of those who did wanted to know *when* they should make a decision about whether to enroll their children at Oak Lawn for the next year. Others simply echoed the comments expressed by board members. The reporter continued jotting notes as people spoke.

No one stayed within the two-minute limit, but Sally felt that given the circumstances, it was best that the board be viewed in a positive way.

The last thing she needed was a bunch of disgruntled parents running around saying the board doesn't listen.

Shortly after 9:00, when Sally perceived that everyone who wanted to address the board had done so, she thanked the parents again and turned her attention back to the board. At that point, most of the parents left the room, but Sally could see through the window, clusters of them standing silhouetted in the parking lot. She hoped they wouldn't ambush her with more questions when the meeting adjourned.

"All right, folks," she began. "We've heard everyone's concerns, so now we need to vote on a course of action. What do you suggest?"

Steve, again the first to speak, was now subdued, partly because others seemed to share his frustration and partly because it was getting late. His mind was already on his 5:30 a.m. drive to work. "I like Rebecca's suggestion that we talk to the authorizer person in charge."

Others nodded. Claudia sat, still trying to absorb the news.

"All right, do you want to put that into the form of a motion?" asked Sally.

"Sure. I move that we appoint our board president and our executive to talk with the head authorizer and report back to the board as quickly as possible."

Without Sally having to ask for a second, Claudia offered one, wanting in part to atone for her tardiness.

"Okay, we have a motion and a second. Is there anymore discussion?"

Everyone looked at each other and then back at Sally.

"All in favor, say aye."

"Aye," said the group in unison.

"Opposed?" Sally asked, feeling the group's fatigue. "Hearing none, motion carried."

"You mentioned a letter. Can we get a copy of it?" asked Claudia.

"Of course—sorry, I forgot," said Sally. "And Paul and I will try tomorrow to make an appointment with our authorizer within the next few days. As soon as we know anything, we'll get the word out for another special board meeting."

Everyone nodded and Sally adjourned the meeting. As she did so, she noticed the reporter stand, ready to intercept her at the door. She figured she may as well be the first to speak.

"Well, you've heard our situation and I'm guessing you'd like to ask me a few questions."

"Yes—"

"I know," said Sally, raising her hand. "If it's all right with you and you're not under too tight of a deadline, I'd like to exchange cards with you with my promise that I'll get back to you within a couple of days."

"I guess that'll work," he said. He wanted to get the story out but he knew it would be better if he had a willing interview. They exchanged cards and Sally flicked the lights off as they left the classroom.

Down the hall, the maintenance man buffed the floor.

Congenial,
but All Business

As Sally and Paul sat in Ted's office waiting for him to enter, she glanced around the room, wondering how one gets to be an authorizer. *As a profession, it's obviously no older than charter schools themselves,* she thought. *Perhaps authorizers are former teachers or principals.*

She studied the photos and degrees on the wall, noting that Ted had a doctorate in education from State. She saw photos of his family, counting what appeared to be four children in one picture, and two grandchildren in another. She made a note of this, thinking that as a family man, Ted would certainly appreciate the trauma of closing a school and forcing kids to move.

"Hello," said Ted as he stepped into his office, hand extended. "Can I get anyone a cup of coffee?" Sally noticed that he was wearing a suit and tie and that his shoes were polished, giving him an appearance as professional as anyone from her own office. And though he smiled warmly, she could tell he was all business. Years of work selling insurance had given her the ability to size people up in an instant.

"Nothing for me, thanks. We just had breakfast," said Sally. After shaking hands, they all sat down. Ted took the lead.

"I appreciate the opportunity to meet with you face to face," he said. Sally sensed his authenticity and immediately liked him for it.

15

"In fact, I wish more board presidents and school leaders would visit. It makes our job a little easier and I think the kids in the schools we charter benefit from such relationships."

Seems reasonable enough, thought Sally, nodding.

"I'm guessing you are here because of the letter informing you of our intent not to renew your charter."

"Yes," said Paul. "And we do appreciate your willingness to meet with us on such short notice. The board met two nights ago and obviously wants to see if there are any other remedies short of closing BPCS. Someone suggested that you might be able to recommend what we should do next."

"But what we first want to understand," added Sally, "is how you arrived at your decision. Sorry to say that until this week, I've never paid much attention to the role of the authorizer. I guess I just took it for granted that our charter would be renewed and that everything was fine."

"Fair enough," replied Ted. "Here's the thing. As you know, BPCS was granted a charter by our organization five years ago. I have a copy of it right here," he added, tapping a thick binder. "What it comes down to is this: A charter is really a performance contract between two parties. In it, you agree to do certain things. If you live up to your end of the agreement, we as the authorizer renew your contract, which grants you the privilege of taxpayer funding as a public school. If not, we're forced to terminate the school's charter.

"The contract has a lot of provisions in it, but when you get down to brass tacks, it comes down to two things: Are the kids learning? And is the taxpayers' money being spent properly?[2] In the case of BPCS, we don't really have any problem with your audits and all that."

Sally smiled, recalling that she had been insistent as a businessperson that *the board of directors select* an independent auditor to ensure that the school's fiscal policies *and* financial decisions were sound. She appreciated

---

2   Jim Goenner, an authorizing colleague whom I referenced in the acknowledgments' section of this book, was the first person I heard use these two criteria to describe the essence of a charter.

earlier than anyone else that financial accountability was crucial for the school. *Whatever other challenges we're facing*, she thought, *at least we got the money part of it right.*

"But," said Ted, "we don't think the kids at BPCS are achieving like they should, something we've been saying to your board for three years."

"What?" Sally exclaimed, jolted by Ted's last sentence. "What do you mean, for three years?"

"Well, we do an annual review of the school's performance. Part of that process involves providing your board with written recommendations for improvement. It's up to you all at that point to decide what to do with those recommendations, but in any case, you are accountable for the outcomes. We've been recommending for three years that BPCS make some *serious* instructional improvements. Your state test scores just don't reflect academic excellence."

"But," Sally pleaded, "the letter I got a few days ago was the first I've *ever* heard that BPCS wasn't up to par."

"I am sorry to hear *that*," said Ted. "But I have copies right here of the previous three letters we sent to your board president." He opened a file and produced the three letters.

Sally was stunned. Not only had Sam failed to bring any of these letters to the board's attention, it dawned on her that given the frequent turnover in BPCS executive directors, none of them had really been around long enough to raise the issue. The most recent executive before Paul had been a great "people person" but had left the school files in shambles. Paul, too, had never seen any of the letters.

At length, Sally asked, "Can you make a copy of those for us?"

"Of course. But as you know, based on the school's track record, we've already submitted our recommendation for non-renewal to our board, which meets next Wednesday."

"Can we attend?" asked Paul.

"Yes," said Ted. "In fact, I recommend that you do. It's a public meeting, besides which, you can request the opportunity to speak to the board."

"We'll be there," Sally said, wishing to herself that she'd taken a more active role in leading the board to develop a relationship with their authorizer. "But can I ask you candidly if it will do any good for us to appeal your recommendation?"

"Renewal or non-renewal decisions are the board's to make. But I can tell you that in the six years that I've been director at this office, they've followed our recommendation in every instance but one."

"And what was that case about?" Sally asked.

"It happened six years ago," said Ted, "right before you started BPCS, and just as I was stepping into the role of director here. I had been a staff member for the three years prior.

"Keep in mind, the chartering environment was quite different at the time. There was much more of an emphasis on just getting charter schools up and running, as opposed to now, where the emphasis has shifted toward quality and accountability.

"Anyway, the school, New Frontiers Academy—I can say their name because it's a matter of public record—was in the same boat as you with respect to student achievement. The school had been failing to show progress for several years. Our board approved a probationary renewal of one year, but one of the conditions of that renewal was pretty stiff."

"What was that?" asked Paul.

"Our board directed us to install a new governing board at NFA. All the existing board members were forced to resign and a new board was created."

"Wow," Sally said, not so much as an exclamation about what happened at NFA, but more in sadness at the thought that BPCS might be able to continue, but that she and the other board members who had put in so many years might be forced to step down. "That is stiff," she said.

"Maybe so," said Ted. "But remember the charter school deal. It's all about accountability. At the end of the day, the board is 100-percent accountable for everything that does or does not happen at the school. From my perspective as an authorizer, it's not about personalities; it's about our obligations to the kids and the taxpayers."

Sally appreciated this, but she never imagined that being accountable as a volunteer board member might result in being removed from serving on the board.

"We'll be there," she said again, rising to shake hands before leaving.

Feeling the Weight
of Accountability

There were nine people seated at the authorizing board table, which faced the audience like a city council or county commission. Paul glanced around the room to see who else was present. There were few others besides he and Sally in the paneled board room, but he recognized a couple of people from the authorizing staff that had been on the recent evaluation team.

Sally and Paul sat attentively as the board worked its way through its agenda. Sally noticed that the board was more businesslike than the BPCS board and that the conversation didn't wander as much. When the authorizing board arrived at the point where the vote whether to renew the BPCS charter was up for discussion, she braced herself.

Ted was speaking to the board. "As you can see from the report in your packets, we are unfortunately recommending non-renewal for this school. Out of the 17 schools we currently authorize across the state, BPCS has consistently scored in the bottom 25 percent when it comes to how the kids do on the state reading and math tests."

Paul hadn't realized this, but he made a mental note of it.

"Each year, as required by your policies, we do a formal evaluation of every school we authorize. For the past three years, as the reports in front of you show, we've sent appropriate documentation to the BPCS board president, recommending various improvements that would bring the school into line with our standards for achievement. And, as indicated by our current evaluation, we think that the school has failed to demonstrate the necessary improvements. We are, therefore, recommending that its charter not be renewed."

The rustle of papers as members of the authorizing board flipped through their reports was the only noise in the room.

Ted continued. "I do want to add this to my report to the board. Last week, at their request, I met with the BPCS board chair, Mrs. Sally Shaw, and the current BPCS executive, Mr. Paul Thomas," he said, gesturing in their direction. "They've both been in their respective positions about a year. Chairperson Shaw informed me that the board had not seen the three previous evaluation letters. They've come today to speak on the school's behalf, if it pleases the board."

"And why is it that the board has not seen the previous evaluations?" asked the authorizer board president, looking over the top of his glasses, without any introductory niceties.

Sally and Paul stood.

"We're not here to offer any excuses," Sally said, figuring that it would be best to match his directness with an equally direct reply. "Bottom line is, our previous board chair held the post for our first four years as a school, but he left the board abruptly last year, saying he had too many other commitments. I won't attempt to answer for him, but I can tell you that until yesterday, no one on our board was even aware that you were conducting annual evaluations. I now realize that as the current board president, I should have been more connected with our authorizer. I accept full responsibility for having failed to do so."

With little hesitation, another authorizer board member spoke. "So, what is it that you want from us today? Is this supposed to impact our decision? I'm looking through the report, and it says that your student performance has been unacceptable for years. Reports or no reports from us, your board should have not only known this, it should have been *ensuring* that the school was achieving."

Sally wasn't sure if he wanted her to answer his questions or if he was making a statement. She decided to reply.

"I agree," she said. Then repeating what Ted told them when they met in his office, she added, "The board is *always* 100-percent accountable and we've failed—and there are no excuses. If you decide to not renew our charter, you will be fully justified in doing so."

"But," she said after pausing, "if there's any way you can see your way clear to give us just one more year, I can assure you that we hear you loud and clear. If we can continue, even on probation, I know we can make the necessary changes. Such a decision would prevent 240 kids from having to change schools. And, in turning things around, BPCS would ultimately fall into the win column for charters everywhere." She tried to avoid sounding like she was overselling her position, but the salesperson always naturally came forth in her.

The president covered the microphone with his hand as the members of the authorizing board turned and deliberated. After several minutes, the board members turned back toward Sally and Paul. The president spoke again.

"We'd like to hear from your administrator, since the success of any school always depends a tremendous amount on the lead staff member. Mr. Thomas," he said, addressing Paul, "would you please share with this board whether you intend to stay on at BPCS if we were to grant a proba-tionary renewal, and if so, what would you do differently?"

Paul liked the board president's no-nonsense style. Like Sally, he decid-ed that his replies would be equally to the point.

"First," he said, "if you grant BPCS a probationary renewal, I will stay. I have felt and continue to feel that there are instructional changes we can implement that will significantly improve the school. During this, my first year at the school, I have been conducting some value-added testing with the children and using the results to get a handle on where we need to improve. As you know, such testing is valuable in designing instruction because it overcomes the primary weakness of the state test, which does not show any child's starting point.

"Second," Paul went on, "I will request authority from my board to make some significant changes in curriculum and staff. As a school leader with a track record of proven results, I feel confident in saying that I can deliver what is needed, but that I need the board to delegate the authority necessary to make some changes. Although I attempted to negotiate this authority when I interviewed, the board, like most, was long-accustomed to reviewing and approving such decisions based on executive recommendations. After much thought, though, I've decided that I cannot be accountable for achieving a given set of outcomes without being delegated commensurate authority to achieve them."

Paul's words caught Sally off guard, but she kept quiet. She had enjoyed being on the curriculum and personnel committees at alternating times in past years and naturally assumed that such functions were part of the purposes of a board. Still, Paul's comment about needing authority in order to be accountable struck her as legitimate.

"Lastly," said Paul, half-turning toward Sally, "I would request that the current board remain in place. As a group, they possess significant institutional knowledge, and my task as executive director would be far more difficult, perhaps impossible, if I had to start over at BPCS with a new board. With that said, we are here to ask for a probationary renewal."

Sally felt some reassurance.

Again, the board members talked with one another for several minutes. Finally, the board president turned back to Paul and Sally. "We are declining your request," he said.

Sally felt like she had been broadsided with a two-by-four.

"But," he continued, "we *are* willing to review a strategic plan, detailing how BPCS would accomplish the necessary improvements at our June 17th meeting."

He paused, looking down at his calendar. "That's about two months from now. If you bring us a viable plan, then, we will consider the request for a one-year probationary renewal. If you choose not to bring a plan, or if you bring us a notebook crammed with bureaucratic nonsense, your charter will not be renewed. Understood?"

"Understood," said Sally, relieved that "declined" wasn't the board's last word.

"Next item of business," the president said, turning back to the agenda.

The Next Step

"**A**nd those were their terms," Sally said, wrapping up her report to the BPCS board of her and Paul's interactions with the authorizing agency. It was 6:30 on Friday evening.

Everyone sat stunned, feeling a mixture of relief and anxiety at the thought of producing a strategic plan in only eight weeks. Because the board had written strategic plans before, pictures of five-inch thick, three-ring binders filled their minds. Even the thought of writing such a plan under normal circumstances seemed overwhelming.

Not only had writing these plans in the past been a lot of work, once they were done, no one ever heard anything more about them. In fact, no one could actually recall where any of the previously written plans were. Claudia said that she thought there might be one stored in her garage somewhere. Rebecca said that she didn't keep copies since they were primarily used by administration. Paul said that he had looked throughout the files at the school, but had been unable to locate any copies.

"Well," said Steve, "what do we do first?" Despite his quick temper, he demonstrated with this remark, that again, he was ready for action.

Sally said, "I honestly don't know. But I'd like our executive director to take the lead in guiding our thinking as a board on this. For one thing, he's the only one here with this kind of experience and besides,

I think what the authorizer board president said is correct. If the school is going to succeed, it is going to depend in large part on what our executive does. Paul?"

Wanting to ease the board's anxiety a bit, Paul said, "Allow me to use poker parlance. I guess you could say we're all in now." Most of the board members chuckled.

"What I mean by that is that we've absolutely nothing to lose at this point and everything to gain with what we do now. The traditional kinds of strategic plans you've written in the past have been cumbersome and—without blaming anyone—haven't really achieved their purpose. If they had, we wouldn't be having this conversation.

"In their place, I'd like to propose a strategic planning model to the board that I've developed during my years as a school leader. I've actually given the model a name: *The Seven Outs*. It's a synthesis of my work in the trenches as an administrator, combined with powerful ideas from some of the best books I've read on the topic, along with some things I learned during my doctoral coursework." Paul was in the process of completing his dissertation.

"Why don't we just pick one of those books you've read and use that?" asked Mark. "I mean, there aren't really any new ideas on a subject like strategic planning, are there? No sense in reinventing the wheel."

"I agree that we shouldn't reinvent the wheel," replied Paul, "but the idea of charter schools is still a fairly new concept. You might know that the first charter school didn't even open its doors until 1992. So, although schools in one form or another have been around for a long time, there really hasn't been a strategic planning 'wheel' yet invented for charter schools."

"Well, can't we just adapt what works from business books, for example, and make it work for us?" said Mark.

"Yes, we could. In fact, many of the components of my model have been adapted from business and other sectors. Remember, though, in the business world, the primary measure of success is profit. Because profit is not our endgame, we have to come at things differently, especially in the early steps of the process."

"I see," said Mark, still unconvinced.

"Wait a second. Where did you come up with the name? What did you call it, *The Seven Outs*?" asked Steve.

"Yes," said Paul. "A funny name. Here's how it happened. I was sitting in my office one day actually doing some writing about strategic planning for charter schools. Within the past couple of years, I had read some extraordinary books on strategic planning, and all that information was starting to take shape in my thinking. I was contemplating how to synthesize some of the critical concepts into a simple, coherent model that charter schools could follow. I believe in the power of the simple. Anyway, I was trying to create a framework."

"Not sure what you mean by framework," said Mark. "Can you give us an example?"

"Sure. One of the most phenomenal books on effective board governance was written by a guy named Dr. John Carver. The title of his first book is *Boards That Make a Difference*. In it, he presents a method for developing and implementing four kinds of policies. When you consider how the four kinds of policies operate together, what you really have is a framework or model for governance. He, too, has a name for his model. He calls it Policy Governance."

"Never heard of it," said Steve.

Paul took this in stride. He knew from years of running schools that board members typically read few books, if any, on how to govern. He sometimes told others that if he had to guess, he thought that kids working in burger joints get more training on how to shovel fries and flip sliders than 90 percent of charter school board members get on how to govern schools.

"Fair enough," said Paul. "But I'll bet you've heard of the golf model, GPS?" Paul knew Steve was passionate about golf.

"Sure," said Steve. "Grip-Posture-Stance. It's a great little acronym that helps you remember everything you need to do as you line up to swing the club."

"Exactly," said Paul. "That's a model, or framework."

At this, Steve sat back in his chair, looking pleased.

"Back to *The Seven Outs*," Paul continued. "After I synthesized the books I had read into seven strategic planning steps, I noticed something in my notes. Several of the steps naturally ended with the word 'out,' as in step one, where the board's task is to 'figure out' where the school is and where it should go, that is, what it is to achieve. As I looked at the steps, I realized that each of the steps could be easily and simply described in simple phrases ending with the word 'out.' I thought, 'Why give the steps more complicated names?' All you have to remember is that in baseball, the team in the field has to get three outs to win the inning. In charter schools, it takes seven outs to win."

"And what are those seven outs?" asked Mark.

"Well, I don't think we have time to go into detail tonight, so let me hold off on answering that until we meet again, if I may."

"Okay," Sally said, "I think we agree with you that we're all in, as you say. And, speaking for myself, I don't watch much baseball, but I'd like to hear more about your seven outs in our next meeting. How about the rest of the board?" she asked.

"As long it doesn't involve writing any more phonebooks, I'll support it" said Steve.

J.J. added, "Paul, you are our paid expert. On a farm, the hired hands do what the farmer tells them. You tell us what we need to do."

Paul chuckled. "I serve at the board's pleasure, so I don't want to be in the position of telling you what to do. But I'll make you all a deal: As representatives of the owners of this farm, if you tell me clearly what you want, I can tell you whether it's doable, how long it will take, and what it will cost. On the other hand, once you've told me what you want and stipulated the parameters within which it is to be achieved, such as budget, I'll need the board to agree not to interfere with my *execution* of it. So, not to take your farm analogy too far, that means that the board agrees not to come back and direct me to stack the hay in a certain way or to make me ask permission to hire who I want to run the milking machine or repair the tractors."

Sally was the first to reply. "Does this mean that we're going to have to start doing some things differently than we have before?" Based on what Paul had said to the authorizer board, she already knew the answer, but she wanted Paul to affirm her question so that she would have it in the minutes that the board agreed.

"Yes," Paul said, "it does mean doing some things differently, particularly with respect to who is responsible for what. Without sorting out details tonight, I'd like to recommend a special training meeting for which I will need about a week to prepare. The sole purpose of that meeting will be to explain *The Seven Outs*, including roles and responsibilities in developing and executing the plan, assuming we're given the chance to execute it."

"A week from today is next Friday and I already know I can't make that," said Mark. "I'm out of town on business for the weekend."

"How about Saturday morning?" suggested J.J. "After the cows are milked, I can spend the morning here. And since it'll be during the day, we won't be rushed and we won't be as tired."

"Does Saturday work for everyone except Mark?" Sally asked.

Everyone nodded in agreement.

"Okay, it's a deal," said Sally. Then turning to Rebecca she added: "Would you please be sure to note in the minutes that tonight the board acknowledged that it understands it is going to have to make some changes in roles and that it agreed to meet a week from tomorrow for training on how to accomplish those changes?"

"Already noted," said Rebecca quietly with a smile.

"Good! See you all next Saturday."

As they rose from the table, Mark said, "Sally, can I have a word in private with you, please?"

Not in the Same Boat

"Sure," said Sally, as everyone else left the room. "What's on your mind?"

"I just don't know about this whole thing," said Mark. "I mean, using a strategic planning model 'invented' by our administrator? And this business of the board agreeing to do things differently, I don't agree with that, either. I serve on the personnel committee, and frankly I think it's a good check and balance to make the executive director submit his personnel decisions for board approval."

"But—"

"And another thing, how was it decided that you and Paul should be the ones to go talk with the authorizing board? I would have fit that into my schedule if I had known about it. I could have come and at least made a show of support for BPCS. I think things are getting off track."

"You didn't get my email?" asked Sally, knowing full well that she had informed the entire board of the meeting.

"I get four dozen emails a day," Mark protested. "I don't recall seeing that one, no."

"Well, here's the thing, Mark. You frequently miss two or three meetings in a row."

"I've got a busy job, you know that," snapped Mark.

33

"I do know that," replied Sally firmly. "But you can't miss as many meetings as you do and then expect to show up and have the whole board recalibrate its decisions to your liking. The board has to oversee the school as a unified group and when you miss meetings, you can't just come back three months later and expect things to be where you left them."

"I disagree. I'm a board member. As such, I have the right to have my opinion weighed just like everyone else on the board."

"Not if you're not here to give it. Look, Mark, we don't need to argue about this. I think you need to make a decision: Either you have time to serve on the board—and by serve, I mean showing up regularly to participate in meetings—or you don't. If you're too busy with work or whatever, no one is going to hold that against you. We're all busy. But you can't have one foot in the boat and the other foot in the water. Either get all the way in and help us row or get out of the boat. And as you can tell from tonight's meeting, we've got to start rowing pretty fast, *and in the same direction*, or there won't be a board to serve on after this school year is up. What do you want to do?"

Sally hadn't meant to give Mark an ultimatum, but she figured that with everything riding on what happened in the next two months, she didn't have any more energy to waste trying to hold Mark's hand on the nights he decided to show up.

Mark was stunned. He'd never seen Sally this direct and he could tell that she wasn't in any mood to play games.

"You know what, then, fine. I'm off the board! I hereby resign, effective immediately."

"Mark, I don't want you to make a snap decision in the heat of the moment. We're both tired and frustrated. All I'm saying is, if you don't have the time it really takes to serve on the board, then there's nothing dishonorable about saying so. But please don't do it like this."

"I don't know who made you the producer of this show," Mark fumed, "but count me out. And you can count on one other thing," Mark added.

"And what's that?" said Sally in no mood to be threatened.

"Our authorizer will be hearing from *me*!"

The Seven Outs

When Saturday morning came around, Paul was surprised when Sally didn't arrive. He hadn't heard from her since the board meeting a week earlier when they set up the training date. At half past the hour, the five board members present decided to go ahead and begin the special training session. Everyone had gotten word of Mark's resignation.

Although they opened the meeting to parents, none came. The board decided that since it was training only and that no specific BPCS business was to be discussed, they would not structure the meeting with minutes, motions, and the like. Rebecca, however, still took notes, though no one asked her to.

Paul began. "I'm pleased that you all took time out of your busy schedules for today's training session. When we met last week, I shared with the board that I have designed a process for strategic planning for charter schools that I call *The Seven Outs*. I know you all are probably wondering what this actually looks like."

"I sure am," said Steve.

"All right, then," said Paul, passing around a handout. "Let's get down to business."

Step One: Figure Out

"The first step in any strategic plan is to *figure out* where you are and where you want to go. If we were navigating a ship, for example, we would need to know our present position and where we wanted to go *before* we could plot a course to get there. In charter schools, this means the board begins the strategic planning process by getting a precise reading on how the school is currently performing. It then determines what kind of performance it desires.

"You can begin this process by asking yourselves some fundamental questions. Often, the most helpful question for the board to begin the figuring out process is to ask: 'Why does our school exist?' You must keep asking until you arrive at a *clear* answer.

"Now, I know that you're probably thinking that sounds ridiculous because you think the school exists to teach children. But not only is this answer incorrect, it is counterproductive to strategic planning. I will show you a much clearer way to correctly answer the question."

All the board members, except Rebecca who was busily writing, frowned slightly. Steve sat with his arms crossed.

"Paul," Deborah finally said, "I hope you're not suggesting that teaching be de-emphasized at BPCS in favor of something else?" As a teacher, Deborah had seen a lot of fads come and go over the years, usually changing with administrators.

"Not at all," said Paul. "In fact, shortly, you'll be able to see that, as a school, we're going to put *more* emphasis on teaching. The point I'm making here is this: Teaching is a *process* that we use to achieve outcomes for students. To say it differently, our school doesn't exist *to teach*, as though it were created for the teachers to have jobs. *We exist that students learn and grow so they can maximize their individual potential.*

"I know that may seem like semantics, but if you stop and think about it, the difference in meaning is phenomenal. *Comprehending the difference has the effect of shifting your entire focus from processes to outcomes.* Once the board recognizes that it should focus on the *outcomes* in strategic planning, it is ready to *figure out* answers to the first three questions necessary to create a plan:

1. What should the students achieve?
2. How well are they achieving at present?
3. How well do we want them to achieve?"

Everyone was contemplating this when Steve said, "So, if I'm tracking with you, the first out in *The Seven Outs* strategic planning model is that our board can't really implement any kind of meaningful plan until it figures out where the school is and what the students are supposed to achieve?"

"Precisely," Paul replied, excited that Steve was already beginning to get it. "And there are two secrets to turbo-charging the figure-out process. One I learned from reading Carver's book, the other from Richard Koch, a business author who has written numerous books, including an international bestseller called *The 80/20 Principle*."

"Hey, I know that book!" exclaimed Steve. "Our CEO had our entire management team read that a year ago. It really changed the way we do business."

"What's it about?" asked Claudia, who read few books.

"Well, it takes some explaining and I'm sure Paul is going to fill us in, but basically, there was an Italian economist who lived around the turn of the 20th century who discovered that 80 percent of the wealth in a country is always owned by a comparatively small percentage of the population, usually about 20 percent of the people. After the guy passed away, other scientists began researching his discovery and they found out this odd relationship applies to a lot of other things when you are comparing two related things. Like in our company, as with many others, 80 percent of our profits come from less than 20 percent of our clients."

"Ha, and I'll bet you guys are a little more attentive to those clients, aren't you?" said Deborah.

"Well, that's the thing. Before the boss had us read that book, we weren't. But when we realized the implications of the 80/20 principle, we decided to do just that—focus less on the smaller customers and more on the group of clients that our CEO calls 'our 20 percenters'—those customers who really make the biggest difference to our bottom line."

"And what happened?" asked Claudia.

"You wouldn't believe it," said Steve. "First, we lost some of the customers from the 80 percent base that generated less than 20 percent of our revenues. But we actually increased our overall profits because the more we paid attention to the needs of our 20 percenters, the more they purchased from us. The next thing we did was to profile them so that we could focus on finding new clients like them. It is amazing."

Then, turning toward Paul, Steve added, "I can see how this helped my company, but what does it have to do with our school? You've already correctly pointed out that BPCS is not in business to make a profit. And we certainly wouldn't want to start ignoring *any* of our customers."

Everyone laughed, including Paul. No one had to say any names, but everyone was thinking how nice it would be to ignore three or four particular families who were perpetual complainers and troublemakers.

"Correct," said Paul. "We won't use the 80/20 principle to ignore parents. But we can use it for strategic planning. *The Seven Outs* encourages the board to focus on a few things that are of vital importance to the school and to ignore most everything else. You begin this process by recognizing that most operational matters—however much fun they may be to discuss—don't qualify as boardroom '20 percenters,' to use Steve's boss's phrase. Another famous economist refers to this as distinguishing between *the vital few and the trivial many.*"[3]

"I guess discussing the kind of playground equipment we want to order would be one of those conversations," offered Claudia, with a hint of disappointment.

"Exactly right," said Steve, starting to assimilate Paul's point. "Selecting playground equipment is not an outcome, nor is it an operational aspect of the school such that the board's involvement with it would add

---

3   In his book, *The 80/20 Principle*, Richard Koch attributes the words, "the vital few and the trivial many," to Joseph Juran, a contemporary of Edward Deming.

disproportionate value to the school. I know you've enjoyed discussing the possibilities, but I think playground equipment is part of a school's trivial many details."

"So," said J.J., "the first turbo-charging secret to the figuring-out step is to recognize that 80 percent of the stuff we've discussed as a board has diverted our focus away from the critical 20 percent, 'the vital few,' as you called them."

"Right," said Paul. "And when you think about it, focusing on everything or too many things really means that you're focused on nothing. Having too many priorities means you have none. It's a self-contradictory statement to say we have three dozen priorities."

"I agree," said Deborah. "One of my mentors used to say that the only time light cuts is when its particles are concentrated into a laser. He used to urge us to 'focus like a laser' on our top one or two priorities. I used to laugh when he said this because I didn't fully get it then, but in view of the 80/20 principle, I think I now understand why he was so insistent. He realized that focusing on the trivial many makes you ineffective. Focusing like a laser means focusing on the vital few."

"Nice word picture," Paul said. "And *if a board focuses on the right four to six outcomes*, you can harness the power of the 80/20 principle to generate some amazingly powerful benefits for the school."

"I'm with you," said Steve. "But considering that there are a jillion details to running a school, *how* do we decide *what* to focus on? Except for Deborah, none of us are educators, so how do we figure out what our vital few goals should be?"

"That's where I come back to turbo-charging secret number two, one of the key ideas I learned from Carver. In his governance model, he calls organizational outcomes that are to be achieved, 'Ends.' I don't want to get hung up on language, so I'm going to just use the word outcomes to describe the same concept. But there is a key insight in Carver's model, one that I think most charter school boards overlook. In order for an outcome to qualify as an 'End' under Carver's framework, it must have three components: a recipient, a benefit, and a relative priority (compared to other outcomes). For the purpose of our conversation, let's just set the third component aside for the time being.

"I appreciate that this might sound a tad academic," continued Paul, "so let me give you a couple of examples of what I mean. A school board might debate at length whether to pay higher than average salaries in order to recruit and retain the best teachers possible. Although there might be merit in such a strategy—and it certainly sounds like it rises to the level of a 20 percenter—establishing 'recruit the best teachers possible' as a board goal would not qualify as an 'Ends' in Carver's model because there is no recipient identified and no benefit mentioned. In such an instance, the board should drill down and ask itself, 'What's the outcome we're trying to achieve?' That might put you in the ballpark where you're actually talking benefits to kids.

"In contrast, suppose a board said, 'all children enrolled for at least one full year will read at or above grade level.' Here, there is a recipient (all the children enrolled for at least one full year) and a benefit (read at or above grade level). That would qualify as an 'Ends'. Now, let's see if we can bring this closer to BPCS."

"I get it," said Steve. "Your 'figure-out step' then sounds like this. Instead of trying to write a plan to do a hundred things—or even a dozen—we can use the 80/20 principle to focus on a small number of outcomes that will have a disproportionately large impact on the school. We then use this Carver guy's thinking to clearly define what those outcomes are, *as opposed to focusing on processes*. And if I'm on the right track, you're saying that unless those outcomes directly benefit the kids, the board is wasting its time because it's focused on the wrong things."

"Couldn't have said it any better myself, Steve. Thanks."

"What do you think our priorities should be for BPCS?" Deborah asked. "For example, we've talked for two years about which program to supplement our reading curriculum with and we still can't decide whether to hire a full-time art teacher."

"Both good examples of things that are not outcomes," said Paul. "But to answer your question, at this stage of the game, the way I see it, we have one priority: Define what level of performance we need to achieve in order to convince our authorizer to grant us a probationary renewal of our charter. And we have less than two months to put a plan together for how our kids are going to begin achieving at that level. This one thing is our 20 percenter, because without that renewal, BPCS kids will go to school somewhere else in the fall, you will each have more free time in the evenings, and I'll be looking for a new job."

"Any ideas how to determine the level at which our authorizer would be convinced?" asked Steve. "Like you said earlier, we have to figure out how good is good enough."

Paul cleared his throat. "In anticipation of that question, I've been doing a little research this week. Using some of the old reports that Sally and I learned had been previously sent to the school by our authorizer, I figured out that for the last three years, the kids at BPCS on average scored in the bottom 25 percent of all the charter schools authorized by our authorizer. And keep in mind that those reports only compare us to their other charters. There are other comparison groups—for example, all other public schools in the state, all charter schools in the state, and so on. For the time being, I propose that we start by focusing on how we compare to other charter schools authorized by our authorizer since they are *comparing us to their other schools*."

"So what's our goal?" asked Steve, growing impatient with all the talk of test scores and quartiles.

"I propose that our goal should be this: In one year, in both reading and math, BPCS kids will be in the top 25 percent of schools our authorizer authorizes."

Everyone sat dazed by the clarity of Paul's pronouncement. Shortly, Steve spoke again. "And how do we do that?"

"A perfect segue to my second out," grinned Paul.

Everyone laughed again, feeling for the first time since they heard the non-renewal news that they might have a shot. On top of that, based on what Paul was saying, Steve thought it sounded like the entire strategic planning process was going to be straightforward and clear-cut. He felt energized, thinking the board could now unite around a single, clear goal that would have more impact on the school than anything else during the next year. And for the first time in weeks, he felt like he was doing something.

Step Two: Find Out

"My second step in *The Seven Outs* process is to *find out*. This is a shorthand way of saying we need to find out how other schools scoring in the top quartile are doing it."

"On that point," Deborah interrupted, "I can tell you that you have to be careful. You can't compare apples to oranges. Some schools have much higher percentages of low socio-economic, urban kids of color, for example. It's not fair to compare them to schools mostly filled with Caucasian kids from middleclass families. Research has shown that family income is highly correlated with student achievement."

Everyone nodded deferentially. Everyone except Paul, who instead asked, "What do you make of the performance of KIPP Academies?"

"What are KIPP Academies?" asked Claudia and Steve, practically simultaneously.

Not waiting for Deborah to respond—for which Deborah was relieved because she didn't know, either—Paul answered.

"Oh, nothing more than the most significant network of urban schools to come along in the past 100 years, at least if it's significant that these schools—there are over fifty of them—routinely blow the state tests out of the water everywhere. If Deborah's argument is correct, then Kipsters—what KIPP students are called—must be from affluent families. But here's the thing: They're not. KIPP Academies are made up of 80 to 90 percent African American and Hispanic students *from poor families*. Obviously then, their achievement *isn't* correlated to family income.

"Of course, the results that KIPP gets fly in the face of conventional wisdom, causing others to notice. I think the first time I noticed them was when I saw them featured on *60 Minutes*. Since then, what they're doing has been talked about by everyone, including Oprah. I guess none of that visibility hurt them either. They've bagged some serious contributions, including a grant in the summer of 2007 for $14.6 million.

"My point is simply this," said Paul. "If the people at KIPP can do it, then other people should be able to do it, too. In fact, others are. There is a network of schools in Connecticut called Achievement First and another network in New York called Uncommon Schools that have adapted KIPP-like models and are achieving the same kind of successes. My concern in comparing BPCS against other schools in our authorizer's portfolio is not that we might have an unfair advantage, but that we might find out just how underperforming we are compared to schools with disadvantaged kids. I know for certain there's a KIPP Academy in that group, and I'll bet you they're not in the bottom quartile with us."

Deborah said nothing. Not only had she not heard of KIPP, she hadn't realized that anyone had ever demonstrated—on a system-wide basis at least—that the so called black-white achievement gap was not an impregnable prison in which economically disadvantaged kids of color have to stay confined. It occurred to her at that moment that charter schools, like some of the KIPP schools, represent an important aspect of social justice. Suddenly, she heard herself asking aloud, "Are there any books in which we could read about KIPP or those other schools?"

"Yes," said Paul. "My favorite is called *No Excuses*. It was written by a husband-and-wife team, Stephan and Abigail Thernstrom. By the way, Abigail was vice chair of the U.S. Commission on Civil Rights. Neither of them are slackers.

"Moreover, reading books about other successful schools is a cheap way for any board to *find out* how other schools have become high achieving."

"So let me take this in a slightly different direction for a moment, if I may," said Steve. "When we were talking last week, Mark raised the issue of not reinventing the strategic planning wheel. You answered by saying, in effect, that one really hasn't been invented for charter schools yet. But here, when you say the board should *find out* how other schools get and stay in the top 25 percent, it sounds like you *are* saying that we shouldn't reinvent the wheel."

"You're right," answered Paul. "That's because when it comes to producing academically successful kids, many schools, some charters, have thoroughly demonstrated what works. For example, if we wanted to find out how to create a world-class high school, we could go visit High Tech High in San Diego. They use a completely different model than KIPP-type schools, but they're one of the top schools in their state, even the country.

"Interestingly, Deborah's caution about comparing schools of different economic composition used to gain traction with educators because we didn't really have many examples of schools that propelled disadvantaged urban children to success. Now, only a handful of academics are still arguing about it. I can tell you though, the people for whom it matters—the parents and their kids in those schools—aren't arguing. They have real opportunities where few or none existed before charter schools.

"From a strategic planning standpoint, once you've figured out what priorities are worth achieving, the fastest, easiest way to accomplish them is to *find out* who is already doing so and how they're doing it, *even if you have to go visit their schools*. The interesting thing about it is that all of these high-achieving schools focus on the same *vital few*: picking the right teachers to teach the right things in the right way, a process that is continuously informed through the right kinds of assessment."

"Well, if we know what works, why are there so many underperforming schools?" asked Steve.

Paul wanted to say something like, *I don't know. Since you all are the ones who've governed the school to the point where it's about to self-destruct, why don't you tell me?* He suppressed this impulse and replied instead, "Lots of reasons, I suppose. In the end, I think most schools are governed by well-intentioned people who simply don't know how to get the job done. I've met a few board members over the years who are simply too self-absorbed with the notion of being in charge that they don't care to educate themselves on good governance. But I think most board members are just relying on the people who were on the board before they, themselves, got there. This leads to a lot of 'we've always done it that way' thinking."

"Seems like these first two 'outs' would be a good starting point for any board," said Deborah, realizing that they had given her more clarity about the direction in which the school should go than she had experienced in all previous board discussions.

"I agree," J.J. said. "In the meantime, let's ask Paul to continue so he can help *us*."

Taking this cue, Paul said, "All right then, two 'outs' down and five to go. In the next step, I'm going to propose something that I think is almost universally overlooked by charter schools in the strategic planning process. It has to do with the fact that our charter status requires us to attract and retain our students in order to get state funding."

Step Three: Scope Out

"I call this third step '*scope out*,' because in this step, the board needs to *scope out* the external environment. This is critical because the external environment is constantly shifting, and when it does, it can impact our school. I liken scoping out the external environment to doing reconnaissance in the Marines." As a former Marine sergeant, Paul enjoyed using his experiences in the Corps as metaphors.

"In reconnaissance, you want to actually avoid engaging the enemy. Instead, the purpose is to gather intelligence about the environment in which your unit will be operating. You're trying to answer questions like: What does the terrain consist of? Are there obstacles between us and our objective? Are the locals friendly? Are there potential choke points where the enemy might easily ambush us? And so on.

"And though I didn't spend any time on ships and submarines, a similar metaphor for scoping out the external environment would be the Navy's use of sonar as part of their navigation systems. Sonar works by emitting sound waves that bounce off objects like rocks and other ships and then return. From these waves, sonar operators can tell how far away things are, etc., producing information from the environment which the vessel's captain then uses to chart a course. Ignoring the external environment would, of course, be perilous. If you were a sub driver, you'd need to know where the underwater mountains are, or the enemy subs that you can't see."

"Good word pictures, Paul," J.J. said, "but I don't think we're going to have anyone shooting at us. What should we be looking for in our external environment?"

"Primarily four things," said Paul. "First, what other schools are operating in our area? By 'our area,' I'm talking about schools that recruit their students from the same population as we do. We'll want to know things like their enrollment, grade configuration, reputation and—for private schools—costs. We also want to know if any of them have construction plans to build a new building or plans to add new programs. Such things could impact our enrollment, which, as far as school viability goes, is our lifeblood. If, for example, we're offering the only full-day kindergarten in the area, it would be critical to know if one of the nearby schools is going to begin offering it. Otherwise, we may unwittingly lose students, something that would be detrimental to first-grade re-enrollment rates, and so on up the chain.

"Second, with respect to the student population itself, we want to keep an eye on the numbers. Overall, are people moving into or out of our area? What are the population projections for our area in the next five to ten years? If the population is growing, how large will the age group served by our school be? In the 1990s, many schools ignored a declining population trend in the external environment and built more buildings. Some suddenly found themselves in budget crises because they didn't have the enrollment necessary to pay for those buildings.

"Third, we want to know our authorizer and to be aware of changes that are occurring in their office. For example: Are there changes in key staff positions? Are they changing any of their reporting requirements? As an authorizer, in what direction are they moving? Increased reporting?

Most are. The point being, what our authorizer does has an impact on our operations.

"Fourth, we need to be aware of what the state is doing. Legislators are talking about new rules for charters all the time. In a few places, the climate is very politically heated with lawsuits and challenges to charters from numerous directions. We can't just sit here within the walls of our school and ignore all of this."

"But what could we actually do if the legislature introduced some new bill that was unfavorable to us?" asked Deborah.

"I don't know," said Paul. "Short of proactively supporting our state charter school association, maybe nothing. But we'll be better off knowing about it as it's happening than finding out about it after the fact. The key here is to understand that our strategic plan has to be constantly tweaked in anticipation of, or in response to, a changing external environment. Operating as though we are in some kind of vacuum will work against us."

"Agreed," said Steve. "I don't know of any successful businesses that would ever think of developing a strategic plan without keeping a close watch on the external environment.

"So, if I can summarize what you've told us thus far," Steve continued, "the first thing we need to do is *figure out* what we want to achieve. But we should be judicious in selecting only a few goals that are vital to our success. Once we've done that, we then need to *find out* how others are achieving the same kinds of things so that we can borrow from what they're already doing and apply that knowledge to our school. Along the way, we need to be continuously *scoping out* the external environment for changes that may impact our school, good or bad. Am I right?"

"Yes."

"Okay, so when do we actually start doing the plan? I mean, you can spend too much time deciding what you want to do, looking around to see how others are doing it, and looking over your shoulder at the external environment. When do we get down to implementing the plan?"

Paul laughed. "I love your focus on getting things done, Steve. Stay with me, because we've got one more step before implementation."

"Let's hear it," said J.J.

Step Four: Write Out

"The fourth step won't surprise anyone," said Paul. "A school should actually *write out* its plan."

"Oh yeah," interjected Steve. "And here's where we get to the phone book. I know all the strategic planning gurus say that if you write your goals down, you're more likely to achieve them. But I'm not sure I see the value in that. I like to just get the job done. I'm with you on *figure out*, *find out*, and *scope out*, but I just don't know that I buy the importance of *writing it out*."

"I appreciate your honesty," said Paul. "But let me explain why it's necessary to write out the plan."

"I knew you would," said Steve, "so go ahead."

"There are three reasons," said Paul. "When you write a strategic plan, you're not so much writing out what has been decided, as you are deciding what you will write. The act of committing words to paper helps your brain think about the topic in a way that it just doesn't when you are merely thinking about the topic. I don't understand why this is; I simply accept that it just is."

"Well, I'm not a writer," said Steve, "and I don't want to be. If you want to write this thing out, more power to you."

"Actually," Paul said, "as the employee who is primarily charged with executing the plan, the duty of writing it out *should* fall to me. The writing process refines my thinking about the best ways to carry out the board's stated desires.

"Besides the benefit of using the writing process to refine our thinking on where we're headed, there are two other major benefits. The first being that a written plan has the advantage of quickly conveying to others what it is we're doing. This benefit alone creates the added advantage of getting the buy-in that we need from others in order to create a world-class school. The second benefit is that it creates a clear map that we can pick up at any point in time and use to establish our bearing or assess our progress. Let me refer to the Marines again.

"When you're in the field, you have what we call a situation map with you, or a sitmap for short. This is a map of the area with key positions marked, such as where enemy units are operating. As you move through the area to your objective, you frequently take out your sitmap and compass and use them to confirm your present position and heading. You can also pass the map around to others in the unit who can see for themselves where you are—an important process should you no longer be able to lead the unit."

"So a written plan is a sitmap. Fair enough," said Steve. "But does it have to be thick? The plans we've written before had to be hauled around in wheelbarrows. In fact," said Steve, turning to J.J., "didn't we have to borrow one from your farm?"

"Yes," grinned J.J., "and I'll need it back."

"No wheelbarrows, I promise," Paul said, as everyone laughed. "Based on my experience, we can write an effective plan in less than fifty pages. Most of the plans I have written in the past using the principles in *The Seven Outs* were less than thirty."

"I like that!" exclaimed Steve. "Heck, I might even agree to read it."

"And once the board has read it and voted to adopt it, we're ready for step five," said Paul.

"I'll bet I know what it is," Steve replied. "I bet you're going to say that we have to carry out the plan. Carry out is step five, isn't it?"

"You got it," Paul said.

Step Five: Carry Out

"Of all the steps involved," Paul began, "step five, *carry out*, is one that many charter schools have great difficulty in doing. Another name for this step would be *the execution of the plan*. The reason, I think, that schools have challenges with it, is, it's one thing to write a plan—even a brilliant one—but it's another thing to actually effectively carry it out."

"Wouldn't that have a lot to do with the ability of the chief administrator?" asked Claudia.

"Yes, it sure does," said Paul, "which is one reason why the board's job of choosing its executive director is a critical task. That person's ability *to execute plans* will be a large predictor of the school's success."

"Are there keys to executing effectively, just as you pointed out keys in the other steps?" asked Steve.

"Yes, but really no magic. It comes down to what an authorizer friend of mine calls 'basic blocking and tackling.'[4] What he means is that to win a football game, you don't need a bunch of brilliant, never-before-conceived-of plays. What you need is for the team to go out and execute basic blocking and tackling, *every* play. *The team that wins is not the one with the best plan; it's the one that can execute their plan the best.*

"There is another key, related to this" continued Paul. "It's in the *carry out* phase of strategic planning that the balance of work between the board and management shifts. Up to this point, the board, with the exception of the actual writing of the plan, does most of the work. You've seen, for example, that it is the board's job to figure out what level of student performance it wants. In other words, it is not the executive director's role to tell the board what level of performance it should accept.

"But I need to stress this point." said Paul. "When it's time to actually carry out the plan, the board plays an evaluation role, *not an execution role.*"

"We don't normally get involved in day-to-day operations anyway," said Steve, inaccurately. "But can you give us some specifics on things the board should avoid in the carry out phase?"

"Certainly. Let me give you the top two," replied Paul.

"Would those be the *vital* two?" asked Steve with a grin.

"Absolutely right," said Paul. "The 80/20 principle applies here, too. Vital issue number one: I need the board's authority to hire, evaluate, and

---

4　This analogy also entered my vocabulary courtesy of Jim Goenner.

terminate, if necessary, all school employees, especially instructional staff. Let me illustrate why. You remember how we talked about the success that KIPP Academies achieve?"

Everyone nodded.

"Well, one of the keys to their achievement is in their philosophy of the principal's job. KIPP believes that accountability must be linked to authority. Thus, a KIPP principal has what amounts to absolute employment and supervisory authority over the faculty and staff. This is authority with accountability, however, because the board holds the principal accountable for the results.

"Bottom line is, if I fail to achieve the goals that the board establishes for the school, the board has to decide whether it has the right administrator. Although there may be times when it's difficult for the board to assess this, one thing is for certain: In *The Seven Outs*, there is no question about who is responsible for producing the outcomes."

"If we agree to that," said Claudia, "then it sounds like you want us to equate the performance of the school with your performance. So if the school performance is in the dumps, then your performance is inadequate, regardless of whatever else you may have accomplished, how hard you may have tried, or how correct your processes may be. Is that what you want?"

"It is not only exactly what I want," answered Paul, "it is the essence of what it means to be in charge. Everyone else in the organization is evaluated on the basis of their individual or team contribution. The person in charge—whether they're called administrator, principal, executive director, CEO, or whatever—is properly judged by evaluating the performance of the organization against predefined criteria."

"Okay," said Steve. "So, if the board says we need to move the school next year from being in the bottom 25 percent to being in the top 25 percent, it's your job as our executive to figure out how to do it and then, do it. If the school doesn't achieve it, then what is the board's response?"

"You evaluate how the school actually performed relative to your stated outcomes and decide whether its actual performance—my performance—is good enough. It's a judgment call on the board's part. This may be difficult, but sometimes leadership is nothing more than the art of making good judgment calls. I'm not saying you have to fire me if we miss the target, but at least we both know what the target is, which will tell us how close we came to hitting it."

"Okay, so no interfering with your staffing decisions," said Claudia. "But you said there were *two* things vital for the board to avoid in terms of roles in the carry out phase. What's the other?"

"Right," said Paul. "The second thing is, at the risk of sounding arrogant, it's best the board doesn't make operational suggestions about *how* to do my job."

"I'm not sure I would agree to that," Steve said quickly. "After all, don't you think the collective wisdom of the board is such that suggestions might be valuable?"

"They might be," said Paul, "but there are three problems with them. First, I cannot tell the difference between a board directive and a board suggestion. This means that whenever you give me a suggestion, I'm going to interpret it as a directive, because I don't think it's plausible for me as your employee to ever come back to the board and say, 'No, I didn't do such-and-such because I thought you were only making a suggestion.'

"The second problem is that once the board makes a suggestion, whether it intended to or not, it shifted the accountability boundaries. For example, let's say the board suggests a certain curriculum. Not wanting to disregard the board's suggestions because I can't distinguish them from directives, I implement it. Then if the reading scores aren't what you said you wanted, who is responsible?"

"I see your point," said J.J. slowly. "We would be partly responsible because we 'suggested' it."

"Yes," agreed Paul, "and in so doing, you would have diminished the board's ability to hold me accountable for the outcome because it may have been skewed by your own involvement."

"Man, I never thought of it like this," conceded Steve. His mind wandered to the innumerable suggestions the board had given the previous executives. He realized at that moment that some of the things for which the board had unfairly held the executives accountable were actually the responsibility of the board for suggesting them.

"Most boards don't," replied Paul, "but if you want to be in the top quartile of all charter schools, you can't be like most boards."

"You said there were three problems with board suggestions?" reminded Claudia.

"Yes, the third is related to the second. So, backing up a bit, not only can I not tell the difference between a board suggestion and a board directive, the board doesn't have the expertise, either educationally or experientially, to make appropriate suggestions anyway. For example, when it comes to curriculum selection, there are considerations that professionals are expected to know about that volunteers are not. Your suggestions may be ill-suited."

"But *I'm* an educator," said Deborah. "Are you saying *I* don't have the expertise to make educational suggestions?"

"Perhaps," said Paul. "I respect the fact that you have classroom experience, but I don't know what your administrative experience is. But even if you have that too, making suggestions runs us right back into the middle of problems one and two—I can't tell the difference and the board needs to hold me accountable for the outcomes. Besides which, a school cannot have two heads. One of us has to be responsible for making the call, and as the board's employee, that responsibility should rightly fall to me."

"Let's say we agree," said Steve. "In terms of accountability, how do we know what we're looking at? I mean, we run into the same problem as with instructional matters—we often don't have the expertise to know what we should be looking at. How do we do that?"

"It's not only a good question," answered Paul, "it's a critical part in the strategic planning process. Let's discuss it as we move on to the next step."

Step Six: Measure Out

"In the *measure out* step," continued Paul, "the board again plays the lead role. By 'measure out,' I mean that the board should evaluate the school's actual performance against the measures that it decided upon during step one. This means the board should measure out the school's performance and determine whether it meets with board satisfaction."

"Ha," said Steve. "Sounds like you had to stretch a little bit to get this step to contain the word 'out.' The step would have meant the same thing if you'd just said 'measure.'"

"You caught me," grinned Paul. "That occurred to me when I was writing, but I really didn't want the model to be six outs plus something else. Work with me on this though, will you?"

Everyone laughed.

"Now," Paul continued, "there are some particular things about measuring the school's success that I want to mention. A lot of times, if you were to sit in on charter school board meetings, the executive's report contains a lot of things that emphasize the past rather than the future, or it emphasizes processes rather than outcomes."

"Come again?" said Steve. "I didn't follow that at all."

"No problem," answered Paul. "To start, let me acknowledge again the work of John Carver and also that of bestselling business author, Jim Collins. In both their writings, they zero in on the idea that progress toward goals is best measured, not by looking at some process that was implemented, but rather by focusing on some indicators that point to being on the right trajectory to achieve the outcomes.

"I can illustrate it like this. Let's say that the board says, 'All graduates of Breezy Palms Charter School will be qualified to enroll in college-level freshman English and algebra without having to take remedial courses.' The board might consider this a worthwhile goal because very high percentages of college students have to take these courses, although they receive no credit toward their college degrees for them. So, let's say, step one, you've *figured out* that this is to be one of the school's most important accomplishments. When it comes time to evaluate how well we're doing on that goal, what kind of things do you want to hear?"

"Easy," said Claudia. "We'd want to hear the percentages of graduates that were able to enroll in college without having to take remedial courses."

"Right," said Paul. "That report would answer it. But, and this is an important question for boards: Wouldn't you really want to know how we're doing before it comes time for students to enroll in college? I mean, after they enroll, it's too late to remedy any problem on our end—at least for that group of kids. So, a key to effective strategic planning is to measure our progress while we're en route to the goal."

"How would you do that?" asked Steve.

"Let me first tell you the wrong way to go about it—which is what most schools do," said Paul. "Most schools would report progress by saying things like, 'we purchased such and such a curriculum that helps kids better prepare for college,' 'we hired a certain percentage of teachers with graduate degrees in math education,' or 'we implemented a new teacher in-service program designed to help teachers orient their curriculum to college.' Now, don't get me wrong. There's nothing wrong with any of those things. It's just that they don't tell the board whether we are on the right trajectory to actually achieve the goal of ensuring that 100 percent of students are ready for college without remedial coursework."

"I think I see what you mean," pondered J.J. "If I set a goal of producing so many gallons of milk on my farm each year, I can't tell how close I'm actually getting by counting the numbers in my herd, the cost of the milking machines we buy, how well the hay crops are doing, or whether the paint on my barn is red."

"Well, I don't know anything about dairy farming," said Paul, "but right off hand, I'd say you probably would want to count the number of gallons you're averaging in a week and then make whatever other adjustments are necessary to bring that production in line with your overall goal."

"I've got openings for farm hands, young man," joked J.J.

Steve said, "I see your point, but we're not producing milk. Isn't academic achievement a bit harder to measure than gallons per week? And what if we had a goal in our plan that said 'All graduates will have an appreciation for the arts.' How would we measure that?"

"Yes, to your first question, Steve," said Paul. "Academic achievement is a bit harder to measure. And an appreciation for the arts is even harder. But here's something John Carver says that I think is brilliant: 'A crude measure of the right thing is better than a precise measure of the wrong thing.' So, I contend that when the board begins measuring processes that occurred, rather than outcomes that are occurring, it is measuring the wrong thing—however precisely those processes may be measured. I'm not saying that the board doesn't need to be informed about those processes—often these things are good to know and fall under the category of governance responsibilities labeled 'being reasonably informed.' But when the board confuses information with evaluation, the school may be off-course without the board's awareness."

"So, what measures would you use for your example goal of college-ready kids?" asked Deborah.

"I'd look to a combination of things like standardized test results, classroom achievement, percentage of kids getting a passing score on AP English and math tests, publications the kids could produce that reflect their skills, and so on. For example, the junior classes at High Tech High publish a field guide every year on the San Diego Harbor. It's a pretty impressive display of their actual ability.

"As an analogy to this," continued Paul, "consider that a Global Positioning System (GPS) estimates your actual position to within a few feet by calculating intersecting lines between you and multiple satellites. Like the GPS system, I'd use a combination of intersecting measures to get a read on how we're doing. Incidentally, the more satellites involved in GPS tracking, the more precise the reading. The same principle works for academic achievement."

"I like what you're saying," said Claudia, "but based on my observations, not many schools do this."

"You're absolutely right, Claudia," said Paul. "Not many do. Maybe that explains why so few schools are truly world-class in their performance."

"Well, speaking for myself," said Steve, "I'm ready for BPCS to become world-class. If that means the board has to begin doing things differently for the sake of the kids, then so be it. What's the seventh step?"

Step Seven: Shout Out

"The seventh step is the easiest one," said Paul. "As we develop and implement the board's plan, we *shout out* our accomplishments to all of our constituents. We can do this through multiple channels. In fact, the more people that know about it, the better off we are. Besides producing an annual report as a school, we should proclaim the achievements of our kids through newsletters, the local media, parent conferences, and so on."

"Got it," said Steve. "Market ourselves."

"Marketing ourselves is part of it. The other part is really about accountability. By reporting out how well we are achieving, we're really saying to our constituents, stakeholders, and owners that we're producing what we said we would produce."

"So, let me pull this all together," concluded Paul. "The *Seven Outs* for strategic planning involve the following processes:

1. Figure Out
2. Find Out
3. Scope Out
4. Write Out
5. Carry Out
6. Measure Out
7. Shout Out

"Does anyone have any more questions?"

"Yup, just one," said Steve. "Who wants to go for lunch?"

Not Sure I Can Do This

"**P**aul, I've got Sally Shaw returning your call on line one. Can you take it?" asked the school's receptionist. Despite the fact that it was Monday morning, or perhaps because of it, things had been hectic as it neared lunchtime.

"Yes, put her through, please." Paul had left a message for Sally on her cell after she missed Saturday's training, and again this morning after he hadn't heard back from her over the weekend.

"Hi Paul," came Sally's voice on the line. "How are you doing?"

"I'm fine," said Paul, "but I'm concerned about how you're doing. You missed Saturday's training, and after I didn't hear back from you, I started getting worried. Is everything okay?"

"Well, no, not really," said Sally. "You know Mark resigned from the board after a conversation he and I had a week and a half ago."

"Yes."

"Well, that, coupled with the fact that I've got a ton of projects going here at the office, is really causing me to rethink my ability to continue committing to the board." The regret in her tone was palpable.

Trying to lighten the moment, Paul said, "It sounds suspiciously like you're saying you don't feel you can go on being board president. Since

I know you don't mean you're thinking of resigning, please tell me what you do mean."

Sally laughed. "I'm afraid that's exactly what I'm saying, Paul. I don't think the school is benefitting from my service on the board and I'm pretty tired, to tell you the truth. Besides, if I was effective at my job as board president, we wouldn't be in the mess we're in with the non-renewal and all that."

"Well, of course you're tired," said Paul. "Who wouldn't be? You've got a full-time paying job, you're a full-time mom, and you're president of a school board. You've earned the right to be tired. But here's the thing—and I'm being deadly serious now. This board needs you, perhaps more than they ever have. And as the school's executive, I need *you* in that role. Is the school facing the challenge of its life with this renewal decision? Yes. Are you partly responsible for that? Yes. But serving on a governing board is a growth process and you're growing. Just look at how much you've learned in the past month."

"You're very kind, Paul. But I just don't think I can go on. I'm not even sure what you mean when you say this board needs me and that you need me in that role."

"By 'this board needs you,' I mean that the ways you've demonstrated leadership in the past month have been critical. Not only have you helped bring cohesion to the group's focus, you also stood firm with Mark when he wasn't fulfilling his responsibilities. By holding him accountable, you've sent a strong message to the board that everyone here has an important role to play. I've had a lot of experience with boards, so you can believe me that sometimes the group is better off losing an individual member who refuses to get with the program than it is to keep running with a weight on its back. And as far as what I need to be successful as an executive, I need what every executive needs: a strong board president who is willing to stand up and lead the board in pursuit of good governance. Sally, you are that president and the way I see it, now is the most critical hour in the school's history for your leadership. We need you to stay."

It was quiet on the other end of the line. "You still there?" asked Paul finally.

"Yes," Sally said. "I can't believe you'd still want me to chair the board after all the school has been through. Are you sure you're not just saying this to make me feel better?"

"In view of the pending non-renewal facing the school, do I seem like I have time to run around with the goal of making board members feel better?" asked Paul. Again attempting to lighten the situation, he added, "When the Titanic was sinking, did the captain run around trying to make people feel better?"

Sally laughed, partly because it was an absurd question and partly because the whole "rearrange the deck chairs while the ship is sinking" thing had been overused by everyone who talks about priorities. "No," she said. "But he did order the band to play music."

"Only because it helped him get people into lifeboats. I need you to keep leading the band to help me get this school into a lifeboat."

"Okay, you win, captain," Sally said. "I'll keep leading the band. How are we doing with the lifeboats?"

"We need to schedule another meeting in about two weeks so the board can approve the strategic plan I'm writing."

"Yes, I heard the training went well and that the board liked your *Seven Outs*. From what I hear, it sounds exactly like the kind of focus we've been lacking as a board since we began. What can I do to help?"

"At this point, nothing," said Paul. "Let me get down to the business of writing. Once I get a draft prepared, in a week or so, let's try to meet so we can do a flyover at 50,000 feet, making sure the terrain looks right."

"You got it," said Sally. "Call me if you need me. And thanks."

"For what?" asked Paul.

"For having the courage to keep leading all of us and this school, even when the chips are down."

"But isn't that what makes a leader a leader?" asked Paul.

In Progress

During the week and a half that followed, Paul worked from home every afternoon. As an experienced executive, he fully appreciated that the 80/20 principle applied every bit as much to his work as it did to the board's. He delegated the supervision of the school during those afternoons to his assistant administrator with instructions that he, Paul, be called only in the event of a situation absolutely necessitating his immediate involvement.

Referencing some of the books he had mentioned to the board during the training session, Paul began writing the strategic plan. As he wrote, he kept hearing the president of the authorizing board in his mind. "If you bring us a notebook crammed with bureaucratic nonsense, your charter will not be renewed." This admonition caused Paul to be concise as he wrote, even though he wasn't naturally prone to writing wordy documents.

On Wednesday of the second week after he started, he put the final pieces of the plan into place. The total length of the plan was seventeen pages, plus a few references, such as websites, where certain information such as enrollment projections had been located.

He and Sally met two days later. Over lunch, he reviewed the plan, while simultaneously using it as an opportunity to educate Sally on *The Seven Outs*. She made a few comments here and there, but on the whole, she thought the plan was remarkably concise and focused. The strategies that Paul intended to use to implement the plan were also articulated, although she now understood that the board's role was primarily to measure the outcomes rather than to approve the processes used by Paul to achieve them.

Paul circulated the plan as an email attachment, asking board members to read and comment back to him within a week. Everyone did so. At the regular board meeting a week later, the board voted unanimously to present the plan to their authorizer.

No one was prepared, however, for what happened next.

Unexpected Outcome

"The next item of business on our agenda," said the authorizing board president, "is consideration of the one-year probationary renewal of the Breezy Palms Charter School contract. The board will recall that when we met two months ago with their board chair and executive, we declined a request at that time to grant a probationary renewal. But we also said that if they would write a strategic plan indicating what they would do differently should we grant them such a renewal, we would reconsider the request. I note that our packets contain the plan they've written. I'd like Mrs. Shaw, their board president, to walk us through it.

"I say this, because I suspect that the actual writing of the plan was done by Mr. Thomas—which is fine, he's their paid professional. But by having Mrs. Shaw explain the plan, we'll find out pretty quickly how well the *board* understands that which it claims to want to oversee. Mrs. Shaw, are you prepared to discuss this plan?"

"Yes, Mr. Board President," said Sally. "Thank you again for the opportunity to speak."

The president gestured that she should proceed.

"First, you are exactly right. Our executive director, Mr. Thomas," she said, motioning toward Paul, "wrote the plan. In fact, he not only wrote the plan, I'm proud to tell you that he developed the model around which the plan was created.

"But while Mr. Thomas wrote it, I can also tell you that this is the board's plan. By that, I mean through Mr. Thomas's approach to strategic planning, something he calls *The Seven Outs*, our board understands its responsibilities like never before. We also now know how we should carry out those responsibilities. The goals in this plan were decided by our board, with the help of Mr. Thomas's guidance.

"I'm not exaggerating to say that as a result of understanding and applying *The Seven Outs*, we're going to do things much differently at Breezy Palms, if given a chance. I'd like to proceed by simultaneously explaining the model to your board, along with how we are applying it in this plan."

Sally then launched into a thorough presentation of the Breezy Palms Charter School strategic plan. She spoke for about twenty-five minutes, covering all seven outs and how each was relevant to the success of the school.

In the end, she said, "In conclusion, I'd like to offer this for the board's consideration. It's true that until now, Breezy Palms Charter School has failed to achieve what it should have. As I acknowledged the last time we were here, the responsibility for this failure rests with the board. But with this plan, not only do I believe we can turn things around for the students at Breezy Palms, I think that we can serve as a model to other schools that are struggling. In view of all that is riding on this decision, I'd like to ask you to grant us a one-year probationary renewal."

"Thank you for your presentation, Mrs. Shaw," said the board president, as sternly as before. Turning to the other board members, he asked, "Does anyone have any questions for Mrs. Shaw or for Mr. Thomas?"

The others indicated that they had none.

"All right, then, give us a few minutes please," the president said as he covered the microphone. As with the meeting two months earlier, Sally was unable to hear the substance of the conversation. After several minutes, the president turned back.

"The board has considered your plan. We are not going to grant the one-year probationary renewal that you have requested."

Before the words even had time to sink in, however, the board president added, "Based on your work, along with Ted's approval, we are going to grant Breezy Palms a two-year probationary renewal on the condition that you agree to adhere to the plan you've written. Speaking for your board, Mrs. Shaw, will you abide by the plan you've put forth?"

Barely able to contain her relief and her excitement, Sally said, "Yes. Absolutely, yes."

When the board president declared that the motion granting the two-year probationary renewal passed, he added, "and we will expect you back here in a year to give us an update."

"We'll be here," said Sally, smiling.

The meeting continued on to other items over the next 45 minutes. Paul and Sally felt as giddy as two teenagers who had been given permission to take their father's car out on a date. As the meeting adjourned, the board president strode casually toward Paul.

"I want to thank you for what you're doing for Breezy Palms Charter School and to congratulate you on developing a nice model," said the president, extending his hand.

"Not at all, sir. It's a privilege," said Paul.

"And," the president added, as though Paul had not responded, "I'd like to schedule a meeting with you at your convenience. Ted and I would be interested in hearing more about how you think we, as an authorizer, might use *The Seven Outs* to guide *our* organization."

"I'd be happy to," said Paul. "You know where you can find me."

PART Two

Applying *The Seven Outs* to Your School

I intended the story of Breezy Palms Charter School to be a kind of worst-case scenario, illustrating what can happen to a school that does not have a sound strategic plan. At the foundation of the story is a board composed of well-intentioned people who have had very little training on what it means to govern a school and thus have little knowledge on which to draw in order to effectively position the school for success. While a work of fiction, the BPCS story represents the kind of actual problems and challenges common to charter schools, regardless of whether their contracts have been renewed or not.

The story leaves the reader to infer that the BPCS board did not use its time to the fullest potential. Early in the story, I mentioned Claudia, who came prepared to continue discussing playground equipment and Steve, a go-getter, who used the better part of several board meetings to organize a shelf-building project. Neither of these things is far-fetched, and neither comes anywhere close to representing the vital few things *a board should discuss*.

In fact, these kinds of discussions are far too prevalent among charter school boards and are not the stuff of governance at all. They are management responsibilities that, at best, should not come before the board, except perhaps as information. A board that doesn't understand its purpose will naturally gravitate to discussing such things because it doesn't know what it *should* discuss.

Thus, the real problems at Breezy Palms Charter School were not only the absence of a viable strategic plan, but a board that didn't understand what its purpose was. Applying *The Seven Outs* can correct some governance deficiencies in that it can help a board realize that its role is to figure out what is to be accomplished and then, evaluate how well those things are being accomplished. **I want to stress, however, that strategic planning as a process is not a substitute for good governance.** In fact, I'd go so far to say that in real life, sloppy governance can unravel the most conceivably effective strategy. Thus, while I want to encourage charter boards to utilize the *Seven Outs* for strategic planning, I also want to urge you to get and keep your governance house in order. You can do the latter through training, reading, and practice.

Lastly, I wish to reemphasize an earlier point: No board using *The Seven Outs* should deceive itself into thinking that it is using Policy Governance. While I freely and gratefully acknowledge the profound influence of John and Miriam Carver on my governance thinking, and note that their influence is reflected in parts of *The Seven Outs*, this book does not explain Policy Governance, nor is it intended to be an alternative.

With that said, let us proceed to examine in further detail the workings of *The Seven Outs*.

Step One: Figure Out

Like the board in the Breezy Palms Charter School story, most charter school boards meet regularly, often monthly, giving at least the appearance of governing the school. But based on my work with boards, many are like BPCS in another way: *Few have succinctly defined the primary purposes of their schools or defined how the board will know when (and how well) the school has accomplished them.* Like Supreme Court Justice Potter Stewart's famous declaration that while he couldn't define pornography, he knew it when he saw it, many charter school boards have never defined what constitutes academic success for their school. They're simply hoping that they will know it when they see it. Such a haphazard approach may work for the Supreme Court, but it will not be effective for charter schools.

The first fundamental, *non-delegable* obligation of the board is to define why the school exists. Once a board has done that, it is capable of moving to the next two steps: prescribing the outcomes the school will accomplish and establishing what level of achievement will demonstrate satisfactory performance of those outcomes.

When a charter school board fails to figure out why the school exists, it creates by default, the problem of having no meaningful benchmarks against which to assess the organization's progress toward its purpose.

There are few abdications of charter school governance responsibilities that are as grave.

Upon reading the above, some readers will believe that their board has defined why the school exists because it has a written mission statement (that the board may not have even written). This might be well and good if the typical mission statement actually proclaimed why the school exists—but most mission statements don't. They are so saturated with processes (e.g., to teach, to educate, to develop, etc.) and verbal ambiguities (e.g., the whole child, a nurturing environment, well rounded, etc.), it's no wonder the board can't govern. It has created what is supposed to be the single clearest point of reference, but in actuality, it has produced something profoundly unclear. Like scouts lost in the woods after dark, the board is reduced to a social group that doesn't even know where its destination is, much less how to get there.

Let me illustrate the problem of unclear mission statements with an example. A commonplace idea worded in various ways in many charter school mission statements is that "the school exists to educate the whole child." Setting aside the pleasant and reasonable sound of the idea, such a statement creates two fundamental problems that shroud strategic planning like a fog concealing the position of a lighthouse.

First, as Policy Governance makes clear, schools don't exist to teach; they exist that children are educated. Though at first blush this may sound like an exercise in parsing words, it is not merely semantics or word games. In the former wording, the school is saying that it exists to engage in a process (teaching). In the latter, the school is saying it exists that some worthwhile results accrue to kids (outcomes).

If a school existed to teach, then the board would evaluate it on how well it carried out various processes (teaching, testing, and curriculum selection) without judging the results. If the school existed that children are educated, the board would evaluate the outcomes (student achievement) without having to spend countless hours focused on processes. Unfortunately, as you may suspect by now, too many charter school boards, if they evaluate their schools at all, evaluate them on processes.

The second problem with the kind of language cited in the example mission statement above is that words like "the whole child" are meaningless because "whole child" is a construct that you can neither measure nor assess. For example, some could argue that people are spiritual beings. If that's true, and if the school's mission is to educate "the whole child," how does the board assess the child's spiritual growth? How about the child's aesthetic growth? How about his or her emotional growth? With an ambiguously worded mission statement, **the board has no way of ever measuring or assessing *how well* the school is performing.**

This is a good place to note that I agree with Jim Collins on the concepts of assessing results. In his monograph, *Why Business Thinking Is Not The Answer: Good to Great and the Social Sectors*, he states, "It doesn't really matter whether you can quantify your results. What matters is that you rigorously assemble *evidence* [italics original]—quantitative or qualitative—to track your progress." Thus, when I refer in this book to measuring results, specifically in *Step Six: Measure Out*, I want to make it clear that I use the word *measure* and *assess* interchangeably. This means that on some results the board assesses, it may legitimately do so using evidence that is not quantitative. (I have much more to say on this in the *Step Six: Measure Out* chapter.)

In sharp contrast to measuring or assessing results, however, is the misguided notion that the board should measure or assess *processes*. This is a serious mistake that can be illustrated with the following examples.

First, let's return to the idea that people are spiritual beings and that the school exists to educate the whole child. A board that assesses processes might be impressed that the Dalai Lama or some other spiritual dignitary visited the school. Or if the goal is aesthetic appreciation, the board might be convinced that the school is achieving its mission in part because of the number of field trips taken to galleries and museums.

Using the two examples above, here are two simple questions to illustrate the futility of measuring or assessing processes instead of outcomes. The questions also illustrate that neither quantitative nor qualitative methods resolve this futility.

1. How many visiting spiritual luminaries are required (quantitative) and of what caliber should they be (qualitative) in order to separate a high-performing charter school from a low-performing one?
2. How many field trips must the school take to art museums (quantitative) and to which ones (qualitative) in order to separate a high-performing charter school from a low-performing one?

Such is the folly of measuring or assessing processes rather than outcomes.

Once your board understands the distinction between processes and outcomes, it is prepared to take its first giant step forward in strategic planning. By defining why your school exists in terms of *benefits to kids* as the intended outcomes (rather than processes), and by defining the performance threshold by which the board will know how well those benefits have accrued (or are accruing), you will accomplish what few charter school boards have even attempted. Again, I stress that unless or until your board understands this distinction and acts upon it, it has not fulfilled the *most basic* of its governance obligations.

Many readers might readily agree at this point, but are wondering how the board actually goes about trying to figure out what is to be accomplished. After all, education and school operations in the modern world are complex endeavors. Where does the board begin?

I wrote this book, in part, precisely for the purpose of helping you answer that question. Remember, I promised you in the introduction that this is a *how-to* book. So, as Julie Andrews sings in the Rodgers and Hammerstein classic *The Sound of Music*, "Let's start at the very beginning, a very good place to start," let's start at the beginning—*how* to establish your outcomes.

How to Begin Strategic Planning

As explained previously, once the board has defined the purpose of its school (in clear language devoid of processes), it must establish the major outcomes that are to be achieved. **These outcomes *need not necessarily be easy*** *to measure or assess;* **they must simply be worthy of the school's resources in pursuing them**. (Again, we will discuss measuring and assessing the kinds of outcomes discussed in this chapter in *Step Six: Measure Out.*)

Recall, too, from the dialogue in the BPCS story that to be effective, the board should generally establish between four to six top outcome priorities. Beyond six, priorities tend to become muddled.

To begin the process, we'll group outcomes according to four different measures or categories. Four measures are required because no single category is capable of capturing the entire range of things the board needs to consider in evaluating school performance. **All measures, regardless of their value, have limitations.**

I've briefly defined each of the four measures below. In the pages that follow, I explain the outcomes relevant to each category in more detail. Alongside each measure, I indicate whether it is quantitative, qualitative, or both.

1. *Relative Performance* (quantitative). This is a rank order measure in which the school's performance (usually) on state tests is ranked against other schools. A school that is in the 63rd percentile rank, for example, scored as good as or better than 63 percent of the schools in the comparison group.

2. *Absolute Performance* (quantitative, usually expressed qualitatively). This is an individual student score on state tests. (There are federal tests that also produce such data, e.g., the National Assessment of Educational Progress, but the schools that participate do not receive any data back because of complex sampling designs needed to generalize the findings to all schools.) Usually the student performance on state tests is reported to the school as being in one of three or four categorical outcomes such as *below basic, basic, proficient,* or *exceeds standards.*

3. *Individual Gains* (quantitative). This is an individual student measure that compares test results between two or more points in time. In other words, there is a starting point in which the

student's performance is benchmarked, and then, a subsequent point at which the student's gains can be measured.

4. *Mission-Specific Outcomes* (quantitative or qualitative, but quite often qualitative). These are school or individual outcomes that are unique to your particular school. They are probably not measured using conventional tests (nor should they necessarily be). They are important because they can reveal information about the school's performance relative to its unique mission that probably cannot be measured or assessed through any of the other three measures.

You can picture the four measures above as a square. By combining information from all four measures, the board will not only know precisely *what* to look at in evaluating the school, it will also have an excellent gauge on *how well* the school is performing along two dimensions: the future and the present. This can be visualized by thinking of each side of the box as a continuum along which performance for that measure is trending in one direction or the other and upon which the board can gauge the school's trajectory. The area created by the box is the school's present performance against the board's defined outcomes (see Figure 1).

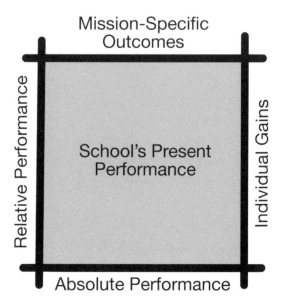

FIGURE 1.   *The Four Measures of School Performance*

The board launches the strategic planning process by figuring out one goal for each of the first three measures and up to three goals in the mission-specific category. Though the process of figuring out what is to be accomplished takes significant time and effort, the clarity that results from simply discussing outcomes will produce what amounts to a rocket flare illuminating the school's destination to everyone.

Given the benefits of that clarity, let's proceed to examine these four measures further, along with some example outcomes a charter school board might consider for each.

Relative Performance

An example of relative performance was presented in the Breezy Palms Charter School story: The school administrator proposed that BPCS move from the bottom quartile to the top quartile in one year. Although this was a purely quantitative outcome and it was limited to one category of measure (relative performance), it was the key to demonstrating to the school's authorizer that it was serious about shedding its mediocre performance. In terms of the 80/20 principle, it was the "20-percenter" that was going to count the most for BPCS's charter renewal.

Setting aside the issue of whether this is too ambitious to achieve in one year (though there are charter school executives who deliver this caliber of performance), the point is that a board should figure out where it wants the school's performance to be *relative to other schools*. Doing so creates a reference point by which the school can compare itself. (It also lays the groundwork for *Step Seven: Shout Out,* in which the school broadcasts its performance.)

To establish where the board wishes the school to perform, it gathers data on its own performance (unless, of course, it is preoperational) and evaluates itself relative to some peer group it has chosen. Some example peer groups whose comparative performance is worth examining are:

- All other charters in your authorizer's portfolio
- All charters in the state

- All conventional public schools in the area
- All conventional public schools in the state

To establish an outcome in this category, the board has to grapple with the important question, "What level of comparative performance is acceptable to us?" Any performance below that level would then be unacceptable. For example, despite whatever else the school may accomplish, would your board be satisfied for the school to perform in the bottom ten percent of all public schools in the state? (Any charter school board that *is* satisfied being in the bottom tenth should seriously ask itself why it deserves continued taxpayer funding.) Instead, I assume that since you're committed to charter schools either as a board member or as an executive director, you want to be somewhere near the top. But where?

During the first three to six years of your school's existence in which the school is finding its legs, I recommend aiming for the top quartile of *all public schools* (i.e., charters and conventional public schools) in your state. Beyond three to six years in the top quartile, the board might want to consider being in the top decile. And here's something to consider: Besides benefiting the kids, once charter schools dominate the top ten percent of all public schools in their states, political opponents of chartering will find it difficult to make their criticisms stick.

Is this a lofty goal? Yes. But for every ten public schools in existence, someone has to perform better than nine of them. Why not yours? Seriously, why not *your* charter school?

While a group comparison number is not the only measure of achievement the board should prescribe, it represents a number that should not be ignored. Without it, an executive or management company can sing sweet songs of academic excellence all day long and the board may not have a clue that they might be singing off key. The building may be state of the art, field trips may be exciting, bulletin boards may be colorfully decorated, and the kids may be all decked out in cute little uniforms (processes). State test scores may even be inching upward (outcomes). But if you're in the bottom quartile of public schools in your state after three years of operation, *your school is not doing the job it was created to do, period.*

I can already hear the objections (from the underperforming schools, of course). "But," some will say, "anytime you have a comparison group, someone has to be at the top and someone has to be at the bottom. Besides, we serve mostly at-risk kids." Let's take these two objections one at a time.

First, when you rank schools, you're forcing a low-to-high comparison. That's the point. Someone is always going to be on the top and someone is always going to be at the bottom. Here's the thing, though: Your board is only accountable for governing the school *you* serve. Don't worry about who will occupy the lower 75 percent! Instead, "focus like a laser"—to quote Joe Overton (see this book's dedication)—on getting and staying in the top quartile as a minimum. Not for bragging rights or arrogance, and not even for the pure satisfaction of performing better than three out of every four schools. Your charter school should be in the top quartile of public schools because *you were granted a charter for the purpose of producing superior achievement.* Let the other schools worry about how they're going to compete with you.

Second, you think your school can't achieve such a standing because you serve poor, at-risk, urban kids of color? (Sadly, a common excuse.) If your board thinks its school performance is limited because you serve these kids, then you need to turn to *Step Two: Find Out.* Your board needs to *find out* how other schools are already doing it, because other schools *are* doing it. As the book by the Thernstroms mentioned in the BPCS story demonstrates, there simply are no excuses for poor performance. Other schools are obliterating the black/white achievement gap. Your charter school can, and should, too. Charters that simply replicate the underperforming schools of many large cities are failing to achieve social justice. These kids are lucky to get one shot out of generational poverty. Don't deprive them of it by making excuses. Figure out what should be accomplished, find out how others are accomplishing it, and then do it.

The point in figuring out the desired relative performance of the school is that your board won't know for certain what constitutes acceptable student achievement if it doesn't know how it stacks up against other schools. It's like measuring fluency in a language: It's relative.

But let's say that you're in the top quartile because everyone else is really lousy. Like placing first in a one-mile race in which *everyone*, including you, finished after 27 minutes, relative performance doesn't necessarily tell you how well you did in an absolute sense. Thus, the board needs to establish a goal for how well the kids will perform *against the criteria being tested*, not just against how well they did relative to everyone else. I refer to this measure as the absolute performance of a student/school, and it is the topic of the next section.

Absolute Performance

Your board needs to determine the absolute performance it wants for each student, usually measured on state tests. As noted, these tests normally consist of thresholds in which the student's performance is gauged against the test criteria itself. The results are quantitative, but are usually reported qualitatively. For example, a student earns a certain score in math by which he or she is deemed *proficient*, but another score for English language arts by which he or she might be deemed *needs improvement*.

In some respects, such tests can be a weak measure of a child's growth and abilities. The results are widely used, however, to assess schools and to inform state and federal education policies and practices.

Like the other three measurement categories, absolute measures provide some needed insight, but by themselves, they are inadequate for assessing a school. There are at least three reasons why this is so. First, they only measure knowledge at a single moment in time (test day) without considering the child's starting point. As such, most tests fail to show student gains (discussed in the next section). Second, since these are usually state tests, the data are not typically reported back to schools in a timely manner that would facilitate the school actually using the results to inform instruction. Lastly, such tests typically fall considerably short of measuring mission-specific outcomes, (i.e., important things that are better assessed through qualitative evidence, rather than paper-and-pencil tests).

These drawbacks notwithstanding, state testing is usually mandatory. At present, the results of state tests are heavily factored into whether a school is said to have achieved Adequate Yearly Progress (AYP) as the *No Child Left Behind Act* currently defines it (see sidebar).

AYP and NCLB:
Alphabet Soup and Political Winds

Some may wonder why I have intentionally omitted much discussion on AYP and NCLB in a book on strategic planning for charter schools. I did so for two reasons. First, charter schools were *not* created to make *adequate* progress; they were created for *superior* progress. In the strategic planning process, the board should obviously set its sights on superior achievement. (Why write a plan aiming at adequate?)

Second, the winds that propel NCLB are primarily political. Hence, the direction NCLB is headed will change as political winds fluctuate. Even as this book goes to press, a presidential election is underway. Irrespective of who wins, the results will unquestionably impact NCLB.

To be sure, the law has produced some value for the public, e.g., providing some transparency in school performance and focusing people's attention on improvement. But I don't know anyone who ever believed a federal law was actually going to result in all children being proficient by 2014.

All this is to say that your board shouldn't structure its desired outcomes around the requirements of NCLB. It should focus on defining superior performance, which, when achieved, will surpass AYP.

Though NCLB requirements will likely change, the board should still figure out what its goals for the school are in terms of the absolute performance of students. *At a minimum*, the board should expect that the school will meet the current AYP threshold (which is an upwardly moving target). The reason this should be the minimum is because the word *adequate* means, well. . . *adequate*. (And any charter school that consistently fails to produce adequate academic results should forfeit its charter. Sounds harsh, I know. But that's the *charter* deal.)

But enough of *adequate*! In the category of absolute performance, as with the other categories, the board needs to figure out what will constitute *excellence*. To figure this out, the board needs to answer the question, "What percentage of our students needs to achieve proficiency in order to constitute the performance we want?"

Remember that absolute performance is only one component of school performance. As with the other measures, the complete picture is created by combining this measure with the other three measures discussed in this chapter. The fact that this measure is, like the others, flawed, is evident in the following: It is very possible to have a school with a high percentage of kids achieving proficiency on state tests but not actually making gains from year to year. The next category captures this aspect of school performance.

Student Gains

In Figure 1, the *student gains* side of the box refers to the academic growth of each individual student. This means that each student has a starting point and a statistically projected finish line. Gains testing is valuable precisely because the finish line is compared with the starting line. As a measurement, this concept is often referred to as *value-added*.

There was a time when such measurement was impossible at the school level. With today's hardware and software computer products, however, it is now possible to measure every individual student's academic growth from one year to the next.

Some schools do this with rigor, using the results to inform their day-to-day instruction. Some schools don't do it at all. In my opinion, most charter schools should. (I do not say *all* charter schools because some, like High Tech High, demonstrate gains using *a combination* of other qualitative measures. If your board chooses not to require value-added testing, however, it still needs to ensure that appropriate growth is soundly demonstrated through other measures.)

The typical way of establishing an outcome for the student gains measure is for the board to determine what percentage of students will achieve a year's worth of growth in exchange for a year's worth of instruction provided by the school. How might the goal be worded? Here's one example:

> *Every* student continuously enrolled in Breezy Palms Charter School for at least a year will achieve at least one year's worth of growth (as measured by XYZ test) in exchange for one year's worth of instruction. (Notice by definition, the goal excludes students who haven't been enrolled for at least a year.)

By the way, as discussed previously, you may observe that this goal aligns with the three components of an Ends Statement as defined in Policy Governance. There is a recipient (every student who is continuously enrolled in Breezy Palms Charter School for a year or longer), there is a benefit (a year's worth of growth as measured by XYZ test), and, as Policy Governance consultant colleagues or board practitioners will have noticed, there is also a relative worth or cost assigned (in exchange for one year's worth of instruction).

I want to emphasize that nowhere in setting this goal (or in setting any of the others) does the board have to become an expert on multiple regression, the statistical method on which value-added testing is based. Nor does it have to try to become an expert in curriculum. It does not have to spend time trying to align instruction with state objectives and standards. In establishing outcomes, it does not have to spend one minute playing amateur school executive, debating the methods as to *how* the goal will be accomplished. **It simply has to figure out what outcomes should be accomplished and how well they should be accomplished.**

In fact, I contend (ardently, as those who have read the things I've written over the years can attest) that the board is making an enormous error, the consequences of which may end up being irrevocable, whenever it crosses over the governance line and begins to prescribe *how* the goals are to be accomplished (except within the boundaries of law, prudence and ethics, to again cite John Carver's thinking).

As with the other three measures, student gains are a necessary component to the board's process of establishing outcomes because they highlight a particular component of achievement that the other three do not. One of the distinct limitations of value-added testing, however, is that it tells you little about other important things you may want to establish, such as outcomes that aren't typically measured quantitatively. This leads us to the topic of the next section, mission-specific outcomes.

Mission-Specific Outcomes

Many opponents of standardized testing (and related measures) object that such instruments are inadequate for the purposes of measuring true learning. There is merit to this objection because students can enjoy any number of the benefits of education without those benefits necessarily lending themselves to quantitative measurement. Thus, a charter school board is wise to also determine mission-specific outcomes in addition to the other goals it establishes. The board will likely evaluate most of these outcomes using qualitative evidence.

I have also given these particular outcomes the name *mission-specific* to emphasize they may differ widely according to the mission of your particular school. For example, there would be obvious differences in mission-specific outcomes for a classical charter school in contrast with a project-based learning charter school, or a charter aimed at redeeming adjudicated youth. Each would undoubtedly have unique mission-specific outcomes.

Let's briefly look at some mission-specific outcomes a board might consider in the process of figuring out what is to be accomplished by the school. In no particular order, I've listed several below. (Again, pay special attention to the fact that these outcomes are not defined by processes.)

- Graduates will possess key skills used by successful entrepreneurs.
- Graduates will be conversationally fluent in Mandarin or French.
- Graduates will know how to use their artistic talents to create wealth for themselves.
- Graduates will be ready for success in college without having to take remedial level English or math.
- Graduates will be literate in the classics.
- Graduates will acquire skills used in real life (i.e., skills that come from doing real-life types of projects, such as knowing how to work as part of a group).
- Graduates will understand why free markets are essential to free societies, as well as each individual's responsibilities in maintaining a government "of the people."
- Students will know how to repair and rebuild the major brands of small engines.
- All students who take an Advanced Placement Test will score at least a "3."
- Juniors will experience travel to a foreign country. (I've already said that field trips are processes but, at the risk of appearing to contradict myself, I think there is something uniquely beneficial about foreign travel that defies further definition. One hundred years ago, it was considered an indicator of a truly educated person. Thus, I would suggest that *the experience* of foreign travel *is a worthwhile outcome in and of itself*.)
- Graduates will successfully complete their probation and enter the workforce with a high school diploma.

To summarize, mission-specific outcomes provide the board with a category for determining important benefits to students that it may not be able to assess quantitatively in other categories. Every school should have mission-specific outcomes. And, like the other outcomes, the board should take the lead in establishing them.

What I Left Out of the Four Measures

Astute readers may have noticed that self-esteem goals, commonly found in mission statements are conspicuous by their absence from these four measurement areas. There are two reasons I never include such goals when working with charter schools.

First, self-esteem is as nebulous a concept as "the whole child." While a healthy self-esteem is desirable (and many kids today struggle with it), I have no idea how you would measure progress in this area, or how much (or what kind of) progress separates a good performance from a poor performance by the school.

The second reason I exclude self-esteem as an outcome is that it generally increases as achievements increase. A board serious about ensuring that its school produces high-value achievements like the kind described above, will, as a matter of course, be raising the self-worth of its kids.

For example, as a result of being enrolled in your school, suppose upon graduation all your students have visited China for two weeks and are conversational in Mandarin. Further suppose that they are proficient enough in math and English that they have been accepted into the colleges of their choice without having to take remedial courses. I think they will be well on their way to feeling like worthwhile individuals.

But what about those whose esteem is still low? Should the board set self-esteem goals so those kids can grow? Granted, some people—usually those with catastrophic childhood experiences such as parental abandonment, abuse, and molestation—suffer from chronic low self-worth that seems unaffected by individual accomplishment—or anything else. What should we do for such kids?

First, recognize that appropriate achievements based on the board's high standards for the school won't make their self-esteem any worse. So don't lower your standards. Love the kids. Encourage them. Build them up. Cheer them on. *But don't lower your standards.*

Second, while your school needs to do all it can to help *all* kids become successful (even the ones with chronic self-worth issues), unless your charter was issued specifically to address this population, your board should focus on achievement. It is fundamentally achievement of the students, not their self-esteem, that your authorizer will gauge in weighing its decision to renew your charter.

Besides, if you do the work of establishing the kinds of meaningful goals discussed in this book, and then evaluating the school's progress compared to those goals, you'll have your work cut out for you, not to mention the fact that kids can feel good about themselves but still be poorly educated.

Pulling the Four Measures Together

So, hypothetically speaking, what might the four measures for a charter school look like when combined into a set of coherent outcomes? To answer this, let's apply what you've learned in the preceding section to Breezy Palms Charter School. As you read the statements below, picture yourself sitting on the board at BPCS:

1. **Relative performance outcome:** As a school, Breezy Palms will perform in the top 25 percent in core subjects of all charter schools authorized by our authorizer.

2. **Individual gains outcome:** Every student enrolled in Breezy Palms for at least a year will achieve a year's worth of gains in core subjects.

3. **Absolute performance outcome:** All students at Breezy Palms who have been enrolled for at least a year will achieve proficiency on state exams in core subjects.

4. **Mission-specific outcome #1:** All graduates of Breezy Palms will be conversationally fluent in Mandarin or French.

5. **Mission-specific outcome #2:** All graduates will be able to use technology to harness the media arts (e.g., layout and design, photography, and sound) to accomplish their personal objectives.

Can you imagine the clarity and the focus this would give your school? The board has stated its primary outcomes in unambiguous terms by selecting measures from the four categories discussed in this chapter. The executive knows what the board expects. If he or she does his or her job, the teachers will know what the board expects (something I discuss further in *Step Five: Carry Out*).

When figuring out what is to be accomplished by the school, however, keep in mind that a school can only realistically focus on four to six primary outcomes in any given year. This is simply another way of saying that if your board creates a laundry list of priorities, then nothing is more important than anything else. A board that simply compiles a laundry list of 25 student outcomes is in essence saying it has no priorities.

To avoid the laundry list, the board should continuously ask itself, "What are the *vital few* outcomes that our school needs to accomplish?" As you answer that question, you are prioritizing your outcomes.

Remember, too, that your administrator may add some goals to those the board has identified. As long as the board's primary outcomes are achieved, and the administrator's goals don't supersede or undermine the board's purposes, this is normal—even desirable. After all, a board probably wouldn't want to say to its executive, "Just produce our outcomes, but nothing else."

Using the 80/20 Principle to Focus on the Vital Few

The 80/20 principle is at the core of figuring out the outcomes to be achieved by the school. This principle provides a remarkably easy way for a board to assess what kinds of outcomes are worthy of its consideration (and in general, whether *any* boardroom topic is worthy of the board's time). A shorthand question that you can use to measure the existence of the 80/20 relationship is, "Are we accountable to the taxpayers to get this right?" If the answer is no, then it probably doesn't qualify as one of the board's vital few.

Though not having the same ramifications as the one above, a similar question the board can ask is, "Will addressing this issue impact getting our charter reauthorized?" Most of the time, only "yes" answers to the question are vital matters that the board needs to discuss. The 80/20 principle comes into play in that only about 20 percent of all the issues surrounding school operations are vital. If the board gets that 20 percent right, the benefits will far exceed the work to produce them.

An interesting thing that can be observed about school boards, however, is that they tend to spend 80 percent or more of their time discussing the *trivial many*. Some of my personal all-time trivial favorites include board discussions about the depth of postholes for a new playground fence, restroom usage schedules, and overflow parking.

Always bear in mind that every boardroom discussion has an opportunity cost. One of the costs of discussing the trivial many is that the board (with its limited resource of time) is failing to discuss the vital few. *If the board is not continuously on guard, the trivial many will push the vital few right off the table.* Don't let this happen at your school. Instead, resolve that your board will focus on the vital few.

By eliminating the trivial many from board discussions, you will have time to seriously grapple with figuring out what is to be accomplished, as well as evaluating how well it is being done (which we discuss in *Step Six: Measure Out*). Focusing on establishing the outcomes described in this chapter should help you steer the board toward the vital few.

As you focus on the vital few for your school, it is highly beneficial to look to the examples of other world-class schools with the goal of replicating their best practices. Finding out how other schools are already achieving terrific outcomes so your school can enjoy the same rewards is the next step in *The Seven Outs*.

Step Two: Find Out

When I explained the premise of *Step Two: Find Out*, to my friend Corey, a successful Australian real estate developer, he said, "Just tell them that when they were in school, they got in trouble for copying what others were doing. In business, you get rewarded."

As Corey astutely observed, entrepreneurial enterprises find out how other businesses have been successful so they can replicate—or at least adapt—the same strategies to their own profit. For some reason, however, many charter schools have been slow in doing this. Regardless, it is merely commonsensical to look at what other wildly successful charter (or other public and/or private) schools are doing in order to see how they are achieving so you can implement those things in your school.

Although the process of finding out what other schools are doing is step two in *The Seven Outs*, some boards, particularly those that are in the initial application phase for a charter, may actually want to make this step one, or at least concurrent with step one.

Of course, before you can go visit other world-class schools, you have to at least have figured out *who* they are. In the process of visiting two or three top-shelf schools (using the criteria discussed in the previous chapter), the board should then be able to begin defining what high achievement will look like in its school. Continue reading for some suggestions as to whom you might consider visiting to begin finding out how others are achieving superior results.

While current research, on the whole, shows that most charter schools perform about the same as conventional public schools, there is no shortage of world-class examples. A short list of my favorites includes (in no particular order): High Tech High (www.hightechhigh.org), KIPP Academies (www.KIPP.org), Achievement First (www.AchievementFirst.org), Uncommon Schools (www.Uncommonschools.org), **along with every other less visible charter school that scores in the top quartile on the their state tests, compared to all public schools in their state (charter or conventional),** *in addition* **to demonstrating fulfillment of mission-specific goals.**

From a quantitative aspect, it's also worth your time to examine schools that have been referred to as "90/90/90." These are schools in which the enrollment is comprised of 90 percent or more minority students, and 90 percent of the children are eligible for the federal government's Free and Reduced Price Lunch program (education's proxy for kids from families in poverty), but in which 90 percent or more of the kids attain high achievement.

Not surprisingly, 90/90/90 Schools have common characteristics in their instructional approaches. To learn what those are, point your browser to The Leadership and Learning Center at www.leadandlearn.com. Enter "90/90/90" in the search box to read a brief case study by Dr. Douglas B. Reeves that describes the practices of 90/90/90 Schools. If you've understood what I've been saying to you in this book, you probably won't be surprised to read that "90/90/90 Schools had a laser-like focus on student achievement."

In addition to this laser-like focus on student achievement, you will notice another common characteristic as you look at other world-class schools. Achievement of the caliber I am describing is part of the fabric of the school's *culture*. Everything the school does, it does intentionally to create that culture.

For example, when Kipsters enter fifth grade—the common starting grade in the KIPP model—they are taught on their very first day to answer,

"What year do you go to college?" And this is no opening day assembly-only ritual. Kipsters will answer that question hundreds, if not thousands of times, before completing the eighth grade (the common ending point for KIPP schools).

From this, you can see that achievement with a focus on going to college is not just a goal to which KIPP Academies give lip service—*it is part of their culture.* And culture works. According to the KIPP website, more than 80 percent of their graduates go to college.

Visiting other schools like KIPP Academies is one of the most beneficial things you can do to improve instruction at your school because it puts you in a position to observe up close what they do, i.e., to find out *how* top-performing schools create cultures which get results.

As you participate in such visits, here are a few other things to keep in mind. I've chosen to use High Tech High as my example because it perfectly illustrates the points I want to make:

1. Don't be overawed by nice facilities. There's nothing wrong with cool buildings, *but buildings do not produce high-performing students.* Yes, schools need appropriate facilities, but these don't have to be architectural wonders. High Tech High started in a renovated Navy warehouse.

2. Recognize that attracting hordes of top talent is easier for schools in highly desirable locations like New York, Florida, and California. If your school is somewhere in between, you may find recruiting more difficult than High Tech High, which is located in Pt. Loma, California, a paradise of beaches, sunshine, and manicured lawns. Of course, it's also a high cost of living area, but that doesn't appear to inhibit HTH's ability to recruit teachers. They receive about 60-100 applicants for every humanities opening. This flood of applicants enables their directors to recruit the best of the best.

3. No school is perfect, but this should not diminish your opinion of them if they are world-class in their achievements. Larry Rosenstock, founding CEO of High Tech High, often says, "We leak oil

every day." This is a poignant way of saying that they have their problems just like any other school. And he's telling the truth.

I recall witnessing an episode of leaking oil on a research visit to HTH two years ago, when a student severely disrupted class, for which he was asked to remove himself from the classroom. His behavior was unacceptable, but it doesn't make High Tech High any less successful, nor should such things prevent you from finding out what the most successful schools are doing and implementing them. Another school executive friend echoes what Larry says: "When you have a couple hundred kids and their parents together, you have everything you need for problems." But don't let the presence of problems dissuade you from implementing those things that work in those schools that are top performers.

Finally, there is another commonality you are likely to observe when you visit world-class schools: There is little turnover in key staff positions, especially that of chief executive. This is more than a happy correlation. This phenomenon exists because *sustained excellence is impossible in the absence of sustained leadership.* Programs do not teach children, people do. And people need leaders.

Let me put my point bluntly: If your board churns through chief executives at a rate of more than one every five to seven years, it is unlikely that you have any chance at cultivating *sustainable* world-class excellence. *The Seven Outs* won't change that. If, on the other hand, your board wants a world-class charter school defined by sustainable achievements, it is imperative not only to recruit a top chief executive, but also *to keep him or her* in that position.

I mention this because the turnover rate in charter school leaders presently appears too high. While I'm not aware of any research on this important topic (if you are, please let me know), from my vantage point as a consultant who works with schools across the country, it appears to me that, on average, charter schools rotate through their executives in three years or less.

If this perception is accurate, that means that in six years, the average charter school has had at least two heads instead of one. In ten years, it will have had three or four instead of two. **If this describes your school, you're at risk of never being anything more than mediocre—at best.** A few schools have *serious* performance problems precisely because of their excessive turnover in executives.

I recall a client school a few years ago that was on something like their eighth executive in what was about their tenth year of operation. Not only did the board fail to comprehend the connection between their exceptionally high turnover in chief executives and their school's substandard performance, it seemed not to understand the relationship between their own dysfunctional governance and the revolving door to their executive's office. In terms of strategic planning, such a school's most vital need is to find and keep a good executive. *Nothing will change until they do.*

As in the case above, a dysfunctional board actually sabotages the school's performance by changing chief executives too often. For this reason, even if it's not as bad as the example cited, a board should regard correcting executive turnover where the school has had an average of more than one for every five years of operation *as its most vital issue.* Anything short of five years is too costly to the school (and I'm not referring to salary costs).

In reading this, some boards may be tempted to accuse me of being "too much in favor of school executives" (whatever that means). Now and then, someone will actually say something like that, apparently without considering how laughable it sounds in view of the breadth of things I have published—to which I now add this book—that are intended to create strong boards. So, I will make my point again so that my intent is clear: Your board cannot *sustain* a world-class school unless you *retain* a high-caliber executive. **When it comes to actually executing the plan (*Step Five: Carry Out*), a capable executive is the single greatest variable that will determine the school's success.**

With respect to the problems that mount in a school as a result of excessive executive turnover, the BPCS story is instructive precisely because it is not all that far-fetched. Like numerous real schools I've encountered, Breezy Palms was on its third executive as it neared the end of its fifth year of operation. As a natural consequence, they had a poor relationship with their authorizer, there were gaps in institutional knowledge, and the school had no overall plan by which a leader could guide the organization. The board was not focused on achievement because its members were content to drift along, staying engrossed in the trivial many. It should hardly have surprised anyone to discover the school was in the bottom quartile. The board never considered it important enough to find out how other schools were achieving and sustaining world-class results. In the end, their charter was on the line.

So it is in real life.

Step Three: Scope Out

In the third step in *The Seven Outs*, the board continues to take the lead in the strategic planning process. The executive may add value to the process of scoping out the external environment, as well, but the board should generally lead because it is likely that it governed the school before the current executive was hired and will govern the school after he or she leaves. This continuity provides a familiarity with the external environment that the executive may not possess. Regardless, it is critical that the board focus on a vital few elements in the external environment that may be strategically important to the school.

There is a significant premise behind scoping out the external environment: *Your school does not operate in a vacuum.* Changing realities outside your school can affect it. In order to effectively position the school for success, it is necessary to integrate those changing realities into your strategic plan. To accomplish this, the board must scope out the external environment.

In business, there is a wide range of variables in the external environment that can affect its profitability (the single primary reason why a business exists). For example, foreign currency exchange rates, market fluctuations, availability of capital, mergers and acquisitions, and stock prices are all external variables that can impact the business for better or worse. Businesses that are successful over the long range, to one degree or another—depending on the type of company—constantly monitor and evaluate those variables. Most of the literature on strategic planning for businesses emphasizes the critical importance of continuously integrating those variables with the company's strategic plan.

Where charter schools are concerned, there are, thankfully, fewer variables, though they are no less important. For ease of understanding, I've divided the external environment for charter schools into two environments: the immediate external environment (where the school is located) and the statewide political environment (where legislative or judicial decisions can impact the school).

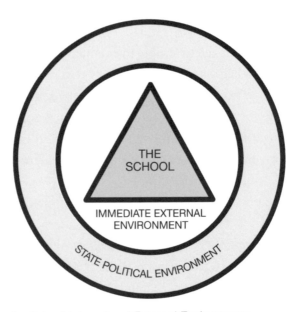

FIGURE 2.   *Charter School Internal and External Environments*

As in business, the charter school external environment is constantly changing, so it is necessary to always keep a watchful eye on it. In other words, you can't just survey the environment one time during strategic planning. You must remain vigilant for changes that are occurring or may occur on the horizon.

In the pages that follow, I will briefly describe a few key components of these two aspects of the external environment, along with their relevance to strategic planning. You can use these as a basic outline for evaluating your external environment, however, you'll have to factor in specific details that are unique to your school. For example, if the local zoning commission has the power to approve your location, it would have to be added to things the board must consider in strategically positioning the school for long-range success.

Your Immediate External Environment

Important elements of the external environment occur in your immediate environment. Because they are external, the board usually has little or no influence on them. As things that strongly impact the school, however, demographic trends, competition, and authorizer relationships must be carefully evaluated. Let's consider each of these three aspects of the immediate environment separately.

Demographic Trends

Because a charter school is dependent on voluntarily attracting and retaining students, the board has to take a businesslike approach to the financial health of the school, starting with the question, "Can the population in our community support another school?" In order to answer this question, the board should evaluate the following kinds of demographic questions:

1. In terms of *overall population*, are the communities from which you draw your enrollment increasing, decreasing, or remaining static? All other considerations aside for the moment, obviously a growing community can support an increase in the number of public schools that serve it. But a community in decline simply may not have the potential for a future enrollment large enough to sustain the school.

2. Based on population indicators (such as new housing starts, etc.), what is the population projection **for the age group served** (or to be served) by your school?

Both of these questions can be evaluated by combining information usually available from your local chamber of commerce with U.S. Census data (www.census.gov).

In addition to evaluating questions such as those above, it is also vital to reevaluate them before you embark on a new construction project or invest in expanding the grades served or the number of campuses operated. Apart from being just good business sense, the board owes it to the people who fund the school—the taxpayers—to ensure that it has exercised due diligence with their money. The board is fulfilling a fundamental accountability issue by answering the question, "Is the potential enrollment in three to five years likely to be large enough to justify the investment for the project under consideration?"

Because charter schools rely on taxpayer dollars to operate, this kind of accountability should always be uppermost in the board's mind. Using other people's money obligates the board to ensure that those dollars are used judiciously. Even in the absence of major capital expansion, the board fulfills this obligation, in part, when it evaluates the demographic trends in the immediate external environment during strategic planning.

Competition

Regardless of whether you find the notion of competition among schools desirable, you *are* in competition for students. But recognizing this doesn't require the board to be adversarial. The board's plans must simply reflect its awareness that a student cannot enroll in two schools at the same time. Thus, if you want students to come to your school, it has to be better than other schools in at least some respects. To be better, the board needs to be aware of what other schools in the area are doing.

You can go beyond awareness to actually appraising the competition in your immediate environment. Here is an example to consider: Are other schools in your area growing at a faster rate than you? The board may want to evaluate why. It may be something beyond your power to change, but all things being equal, good schools grow faster than mediocre ones. If you are losing enrollment to other schools, you should definitely evaluate why.

Again, the focus is not on growth for growth's sake, though enrollment growth is generally a good thing. It means more revenue for your school, particularly if the enrollment is evenly distributed over existing grades. (For example, three more fifth graders where the enrollment is already 22 is probably a more desirable scenario than seven more. By adding the three to the existing class, bringing it to 25 students, the school increases its revenues without substantially increasing its expenses. The executive could split the latter group into two sections of 14 and 15 each, but this raises overhead costs because you have to hire an additional teacher.)

The point being, beyond some minimal enrollment threshold necessary to operate in the black, enrollment growth should never be viewed as a goal in and of itself. It is better viewed as the byproduct of achievement, meaning that your school is performing so well that it is growing. People want to be there because of what you accomplish in the lives of kids. Thankfully, however, student achievement is not dependent on a large student body. If it were, all the large schools in your environment would automatically be good schools. Obviously, this is not the case.

Beyond enrollment trends, I recommend scoping out the following pieces of information about other schools operating in the same recruitment area. I recommend that you also include private day schools that recruit from the same area as you in your analysis of the immediate external environment. (The enrollment in private boarding schools usually comes from outside of the immediate area, so you likely needn't appraise their impact on your school.) Here's a quick list of things to know about other schools in your area:

1. Name and location
2. Grades served/enrollment
3. Distinctive characteristics (awards won, instructional focus, etc.)
4. Overall academic performance, *especially compared to your school*

5. General reputation in the community
6. Tuition costs (for private schools)

Once you have gathered this information (which a board committee can easily do), create a plot map that can help your board visualize the impact of these schools in your immediate environment. To do this, follow the steps below.

First, choose a single color of push pin (e.g., yellow). On a map of your area, insert a yellow pin depicting each school's location. Use a green pin to mark your own location.

Now, to the best of your ability, draw circles around each school pin, estimating the area from which they draw their enrollment. These schools are the primary competition in your immediate environment.

Next, print out the ZIP code of each family enrolled in your school (or home address list for smaller schools that draw from one or two ZIP code areas only). Insert red push pins to depict each family's location.

Now, look at the way the pins are distributed on the map. Does your enrollment come from any predominant area? Why? Where do the outliers—the people who travel the farthest to use your school—come from? Why do they come that far? If there are other schools they could have chosen located between you and them (which should be visible on your plot map), you might learn something valuable about your school by asking those families why they chose yours.

Keep in mind that it is inadequate to measure these data points just once. Because conditions in the immediate environment are constantly shifting, it is necessary for you to stay on top of things. That school across town that represented no competition to your enrollment last year might have altered a significant program, such as adding a full-day kindergarten where they previously offered only a half-day. Your strategic plan will be more effective as you factor in such changes in your immediate environment.

Authorizer Relationship

In many states, local districts authorize most or all charter schools (e.g., California, Oregon, Florida). Other states have authorizers with the authority to authorize schools throughout the state (e.g., Michigan, Arizona, New York). Although the political ramifications of the former are beyond the scope of this book, the board's relationship with its authorizer is crucial.

Regardless of the scenario in your state, I include the aspect of a charter school's authorizer relationship under the heading of the immediate environment for the simple reason that even if you are authorized by a statewide authorizing entity that is not in close geographic proximity to your school, what your authorizer is doing typically has the same level of impact on your school *as though it were in your immediate area.*

The last thing you want is to be like the board of Breezy Palms, which didn't even know its authorizer. Here are a few points to consider in thinking about your authorizer relationship.

First, it is clear that some authorizers behave as political adversaries of the schools they authorize. Under such circumstances, about the most you can do is your best in maintaining a professional relationship. Use a competent board attorney, if necessary, to communicate in difficult situations. Even if the authorizer is adversarial, the expression, "Keep your friends close and your enemies closer" is valuable for a reason. (Editor's note: Although this is sometimes attributed to Sun Tzu, and sometimes Machiavelli, [the quote] seems to be original to Michael Corleone in *The Godfather.*)

But keep in mind that the 80/20 principle probably applies in such situations. It's likely that only 20 percent of the people that comprise the authorizing agency (or fewer) create 80 percent of the adversarial tension. Because of this, sometimes a board election or administrative change resulting in the departure of just one or two people can completely change the dynamics of the authorizing relationship. Keep the faith and maintain good relationships with as many people as possible so that when that day comes, your school will be in the best possible position.

With that said, however, I've observed many situations in which the school acted as though the authorizer was being hostile, but in reality, the authorizer was simply doing the job it was created to do. As in the BPCS story, the authorizer had no intent on being in an adversarial relationship with the school (despite the fact that one or more board members incorrectly perceived them that way). By recommending non-renewal of their charter, the authorizer was simply doing its job. Remember that, like the school itself, the authorizer has an obligation to the taxpayers. If the authorizer is to objectively fulfill those obligations, sooner or later it will likely have to close one or more charter schools.

One final word about authorizer relationships: I've noticed that some boards delegate this to their executive director or the management company they've hired. While it is necessary for management to maintain a professional relationship with the authorizer, the entire responsibility for doing so should never be delegated. *The board should maintain its own direct line with the authorizer.* Such communications help ensure that the board is directly hearing the authorizer's position. That way, if there are problems with the school's performance or reporting, *the board* has a direct link with the organization that is ultimately charged with assessing the school's performance and making a renewal decision.

A monthly phone call from the board president to the authorizer is enough to begin developing this relationship. Along these lines, I was impressed by something an authorizer executive friend of mine recently said at a conference. He was presenting a workshop to board members of various schools on his responsibilities as an authorizer and said that only one individual called him on a monthly basis to inquire about how things were going from his perspective. Can you believe that? Out of the dozens of schools his agency authorizes, only one individual calls him on a regular basis!

You may think that a monthly call from the board president to the authorizer is too much work. If so, keep in mind, that of all the things in the immediate environment that can impact your school, the authorizer's position on any number of things can be critical.

Your State Political Environment

The second key consideration in the external environment is what I call *the general chartering climate* in your state. Well before the advent of charter schools, public schools were highly politicized. Unions, lawsuits, contested election results, and media influences are all inevitable in any endeavor annually funded by a half-trillion dollars of taxpayers' money. Charter schools, in a broad sense, cut across the grain of existing power bases, money control, and jobs. Hence, they ratchet up several more notches the politicization of public schools.

In some states, charter schools are largely accepted for what they are: public school choices. In such states, there are no artificial caps limiting growth of schools or enrollment, funding is largely equitable, and schools can operate multiple campuses. But in other states, the attacks in both the courts and the legislatures are fierce and unrelenting. Having a good handle on the climate in your state is an essential part of developing a sound strategy.

You may be aware of these things, but think there's nothing you can do to shape events at the state level. Not so. There are *a few vital activities* that your board can establish to influence the political chartering climate in your state. I discussed the most vital of these in *Step One: Figure Out*, when I said that political opposition will be considerably reduced once most charter schools outperform their conventional public school counterparts. Beyond doing so, consider the following.

At a minimum, your school should support the development of a strong state association which, when operating properly, is an invaluable coalition through which your school can make its voice heard in the political arena. A strong association will also help keep your board informed of those things that are taking place in the legislature or the courts that may impact your school.

By "support the development of," I mean that in addition to paying whatever membership dues are necessary, the board should allocate funds for your entire school (including board members) to attend the state convention, stay connected with the leadership of that association, and make additional contributions for court battles as may be necessary from time to time. This is part of strategically positioning your school to be part of a larger successful charter constellation.

In conjunction with supporting the development of a strong state association, the board can be the connection through which the school continuously educates the parents it serves. Many parents still don't understand how charter schools are different from conventional public schools or that charter schools are under assault. And as the state association is likely a nonprofit organization in need of operating dollars, the board holds a position of credibility from which it can educate the school's parents about the value of making individual tax-deductible contributions.

Without such efforts on your part, most of the parents in your school will be unaware of the crucial role played by the association that is ultimately working for them. Even if they are aware that the organization exists (which they usually aren't), they probably, at best, have only a vague notion how it represents *their interests* on a statewide level. As the local board, you can open doors to the parents in your school on behalf of the state association. Don't wait until there is some impending piece of damaging legislation or nefarious lawsuit to do this.

If evaluating the external environment doesn't seem glamorous or worthwhile in the governance or management process of a charter school, consider that no successful business enterprise operates in ignorance of it—at least, not for long.

Step Four: Write Out

In this phase of strategic planning, the primary role now shifts to the executive, as it did in the BPCS story. Up to this point, the board has taken the lead in figuring out what it wants, finding out how others are already achieving it, and scoping out the external environment for things that may impact the school's position. As the environment changes, the board may want or need to recalibrate what it wants to achieve. (To varying degrees, the first three steps of *The Seven Outs* often take place in the process of applying or reapplying for a charter.)

Once the board has formulated a complete picture of what the school will achieve, how others are doing it, and what the immediate environment is like, it has arrived at a turning point in strategic planning.

To proceed, the board will need professional expertise: It will need an executive director, i.e., someone who *executes* the board's intent. I usually refer to this person as the executive, executive director, or CEO, rather than administrator, principal, school leader, or other title, in order to emphasize the skill at which this leader must excel. Because the board cannot be onsite *and* it does not possess school operations expertise, it must delegate the authority for achieving its goals to an executive.

Admittedly, successfully navigating the board-executive relationship can be complex at times—as in, when trying to determine who's responsible for what. But as discussed in *Step Two: Scope Out* in which it was noted that high-performing schools retain their executives, getting the board-executive relationship right is essential to producing and *sustaining* effective outcomes for the school.

To help clarify this board-executive relationship in strategic planning, I again draw upon a metaphor. Happily, while I was writing this book, a television documentary offered the perfect one: how Rolls Royce automobiles are made.

Prior to seeing the show, I was unaware that each car is custom made. The program explained how every car is an engineering masterpiece, uniquely designed by each individual owner. What was particularly interesting was that the entire process could be conceived of as a variation of *The Seven Outs*.

The process begins when the owner of the Rolls meets with a design team to *figure out* the specifications desired, such as color, interior fabric, wood and metal trim designs, and engine size. A professional team guides the owner through the process. Of course, part of the process includes showing the owner other Rolls Royce cars so he or she can *find out* what other owners have done. The design process even includes, believe it or not, the *scoping out* of the external environment—the kinds of roads upon which the owner will operate and the conditions in which he or she will most often drive.

Once the owner has prescribed all the specifications, the professionals begin the manufacturing process, a process the owner lacks the expertise to guide or control. The extent to which he or she may supervise it is only in conjunction with ensuring that he or she is satisfied with the *outcomes*. Imagine the fiasco that would result if the owners tried telling the manufacturer *how* to build the car.

Granted, this is an imperfect metaphor—leading a school is a far more complex operation than manufacturing a car—but you get my point.

Beyond the expertise required to determine how to translate the board's intent (i.e., the four to six intended outcomes that the board figured out it wants the school to achieve) into a viable operational plan, there are three reasons why the executive should actually be the one to write out the plan.

The first reason is that once the board has figured out what it wants to achieve and has taken the time to find out how others are doing it, a strategic plan is mostly about processes. To determine these, the board needs an expert—the school's executive director.

For example, let's say the board decides that all children will read at or above grade level. To understand how this outcome occurs, it has visited other schools where at least 90 percent of the kids are proficient in reading. In having done so, it is likely that it observed that there is a laser like focus on phonics (for decoding) and that reading content is substantive (for comprehension). They are also likely to have observed that such schools utilize some form of continuous assessment, the results of which then further inform instruction. (This process is sometimes referred to as *data-driven decision making*, however, I think of it as a *leadership-driven* process in which data *informs* decision making.)

The right executive possesses the knowledge and skills (or is in the process of acquiring them) to implement various processes to produce the right outcomes. He or she knows how to select the best reading curricula, the best supplemental materials to augment it with, what kind of testing to conduct, and the intervals at which to conduct it. Skilled executives also know which characteristics to look for in teachers, along with how to coach and develop them.

In contrast, it would generally be impossible for a board to acquire the level of expertise necessary to implement these processes, so it delegates authority to its executive while holding him or her accountable for the outcomes. The executive thinks through the processes while writing the strategic plan.

The second reason the executive writes the plan is, that at its core, writing is really a thinking process. This is to say that the action of getting words out of your head and onto paper is valuable in and of itself *because it requires you to think*. My experience as an executive and author has been the same as that of historian Daniel J. Boorstin when he said, "I write to discover what I think."

When an executive writes out a strategic plan, as Paul did in the story, critical thinking about the process and content will naturally occur. Writing will trigger thoughts that must be integrated into the plan. For example, in thinking about how one might raise reading comprehension scores, many considerations come to mind. The executive might have to make a personnel change, augment or change the curricula, adjust the school's daily schedule, create a task force to examine state-mandated objectives, and so on. Writing out the process strategy actually helps the executive formulate it.

The third key reason the executive should write the plan is similar to the Rolls Royce illustration. Once the board has established what is to be accomplished by the school, it must yield school operations to a person with the expertise to accomplish it: the executive. It's logical, then, that since the executive is accountable to the board for executing the board's desires, he or she should be the person who has the authority to determine the plan for *how* the school will achieve them. A board severely diminishes the capacity of its executive director when it delegates to him or her less authority than that typically possessed by a convenience store manager.

A Framework for the Plan

The executive must take the board's priorities, add his or her own to them (provided that they augment rather than supersede or contradict), and then synthesize them *into a series of operational steps*. In other words, the executive must know how to translate intent into a plan and then follow with actions that will accomplish it.

What should be in that plan? Essentially three components, described as follows:

> *Personnel.* If world-class achievement is what the board has in mind, then it is imperative that the executive recruit and *retain* the best

teachers. The plan should demonstrate that the executive has thought through how that will be best accomplished. It should factor in things like the executive's strategy for professional growth and renewal of faculty. It should also contain nuts-and-bolts things directly related to staffing patterns, such as teacher-to-student ratio, grade configuration (i.e., one section or two of a particular grade), and compensation/performance bonus plans.

Just how important is it to get the right people in a school? Famed business researcher and author Jim Collins refers to the personnel strategy of great organizations as getting "the right people on the bus." Considering that the quality of the teacher in the classroom *is* the primary determinant of student achievement, charter school executives must obsess over getting the best teachers the school can afford. The executive must continuously ask himself or herself, "Do I have the right people? If so, do I have them in the right classrooms?" (As difficult as it may sometimes be to answer these questions, it's part of the responsibility an executive must shoulder.)

Operations. The main consideration of the operations component is the budget by which the school functions in pursuit of the board's goals. Other things may need to be addressed, however, *operational discussion in the plan should be limited to those things that directly influence the accomplishment of the board's directives.* (Remember, that part of the goal of *The Seven Outs* is to produce a concise, readable plan. This naturally precludes writing about every operational detail that could be included.)

Mission Fulfillment. This part of the plan addresses the decisions the executive is going to make concerning things like curriculum, assessment, and instructional philosophy that achieve the board's goals. Because of the highly regulated environment of charters, the executive should also discuss how he or she plans to achieve state learning objectives (called by different names in various states). Care should be taken, however, not to be too technical in this section. The goal is to focus on how the board's outcomes will be achieved.

It is imperative that each of these three components be integrated with the other. For example, recruiting and retaining the best teachers is the key to fulfilling the mission component. Because talent costs, however, recruiting the best teachers also has enormous budget ramifications. The executive's challenge is in determining how to best integrate the components.

And, as explained in *Step Three: Scope Out*, the school does not operate in a vacuum. There is both an immediate external environment and a state external environment that impact the school. This necessitates integrating into the plan what is occurring, or predicted to occur, in the external environment. For example, if there are two new charter schools being opened in your community, that fact should be integrated into the plan.

The three main components of a charter school strategic plan, along with the layered external environment (the relevant aspects of which were discussed in *Step Three: Scope Out*), are pictured in Figure 3 below.

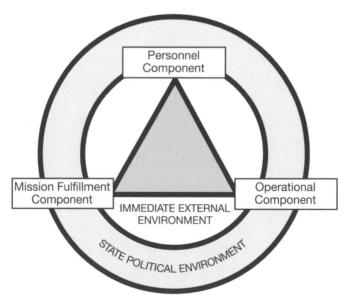

FIGURE 3.   *The Three Components of School Operations in a Layered External Environment*

In writing out the plan, the school executive must determine *how* to answer the questions pertinent to each component because he or she will be accountable to the board for the results, good or bad. If the board interferes in the planning process by inserting itself into personnel decisions, for example, *it diminishes its own capacity to hold the executive accountable for the results.*

Lastly, when the plan is complete, it is the executive who is charged with executing the plan—the next step.

A Word to School Executives: Make Time to Think

"Action drives out thought."
—Richard Koch

Running schools—I did it for twelve years—is a harried job. You have little control over a typical day, such as when a student discipline problem arises that requires your involvement. As you know, *a single such circumstance* can take a half day, or longer, to resolve, thus obliterating every other minute you had scheduled for other things.

Because of this, if not intentionally planned, having time to think often gets crowded out. If it occurs at all, it usually gets tucked in around the edges of your calendar, e.g., driving to and from school—which is not quality time.

Yet, of all the activities that are among *the vital few* to your effectiveness as a school leader, thinking is one of a handful of the "20 percenters." This means that, in terms of benefits derived from all the uses of your time in leading a school, thinking is one of a few things that can produce far more impact than 80 percent of everything else you spend time doing.

continues ▶

With this in mind, do yourself—and your school—a huge favor: Set aside one morning or afternoon *every* week, or less than 10 percent of a 50-hour week, for thinking. (I do not recommend evening hours for serious thinking because human energy is cyclical and most people are beginning to wind down after 5 or 6 p.m.)

Thinking time is just that. It's not for conferencing, working out, or goofing off (though some people may mistake it for that)—it's for thinking.

The following guidelines can help you structure your thinking time to be the most effective:

1. Your best ideas will occur to you when you are relaxed, so it is imperative that you go to places you find relaxing (i.e., the woods, the pool or beach, your deck, the coffee shop, etc.) to do your thinking. I'm serious. My best ideas for articles, books, and presentations—my "20 percenters"—come to me when I'm sitting beside a pool or at my favorite coffee shop. Unless you find your office space quiet and inspirational *and* people will refrain from interrupting you when you ask them not to, you need to leave campus. (On the other hand, if your office has a serene view of the mountains or a lake and you can relax, you can stay there.) One extraordinarily successful charter school executive I know has an unusual, but effective strategy for preserving time to think. When she first told me that she spends several hours each week cutting the school's grass, I thought to myself that she might not be using her time to its maximum potential. But when she told me that no one interrupts her and that the riding mower drowns out all the noise around her, I immediately realized why she cuts the grass: *She is making time to think*. I'd rather lie in a hammock sipping an iced tea, but hey, each to his or her own. Go where your best ideas have come to you in the past.

2. Appoint a responsible person to be in charge of the campus(es) in your absence. Make sure this person understands he or she is in charge and that everyone else understands it, too. In other words, no "straw boss" delegation. This confuses people, ultimately interrupting your thinking time.

3. Turn your handheld device or cell phone OFF (otherwise you'll be tempted to look at the caller ID). Short of an emergency evacuation or some such catastrophe, there is nothing that will take place at your school that can't wait four hours for you to respond. A fellow school executive used to say it like this: "If your school can't function without you for an afternoon, you're not leading well." He was right. If you allow for the possibility of interruptions, you will be interrupted. In contrast, ask your staff to simply respond to anyone inquiring for you during your absence with, "I'm sorry, he isn't available right now. I'll be glad to help you, or I can take a message."

4. Keep a journal in which to jot down your ideas and thoughts, but do not bring reading material unless it is directly related to a problem you are trying to solve or a goal you are trying to accomplish. Even then, make sure you are doing more thinking than reading.

5. Sometimes I find it helpful to bring my calendar. This allows me to plan and review critical dates. Be careful, however, that the entire thinking block doesn't get consumed with normal scheduling activities, for which you should reserve other times.

In addition to incorporating this practice of setting aside thinking time into your leadership, it's also valuable to cultivate the discipline of allocating time for thinking in your subordinates, particularly executives who report directly to you. They will be observing your actions and practices anyway, so go ahead and

continues ▶

openly model the discipline while simultaneously cultivating it in your colleagues. That's the essence of leadership.

Most boards will support their executive in pursuit of time to think, but I've no doubt that some school executives reading this book work for boards that won't. Boards like the latter tend to misunderstand their role by thinking of themselves (usually individually) as the executive's senior managers. Board members themselves may not understand that thinking is one of the vital few activities necessary for sound leadership.

If this describes your current situation, try to help the board understand that the school will benefit. If the board still impedes you or even goes so far as to direct you as to how you should manage your day, consider that there are other charter schools you can lead. Wherever you land though, you need time to think, so it may be a useful point to discuss during interviews.

I cannot overemphasize the importance of thinking as a leadership discipline. Incorporating this discipline into our lives is sometimes difficult in a culture such as ours that emphasizes *doing*. I don't want to understate the value of doing, but when it occurs without adequate forethought, the results will not be as effective.

In contrast, if you harness the power of the 80/20 principle by using 10-20 percent of your work week for thinking, you will experience renewed energy, an increased focus, and greater effectiveness as a leader. If those were the only three benefits, it would be worth the investment of your time.

Step Five: Carry Out

As previously noted, the very title of executive contains the implied essence of the job—one who executes a plan. Thus, as the logical next step to writing the plan, the executive must also take the lead in the fifth step of the strategic planning process: he or she must *carry out* the plan.

Having the ability to carry out a plan, even though it will involve countless changes along the way, is a hallmark of a charter school executive. A brilliantly devised plan—even one with pictures that is professionally bound with a four-color cover—is worthless if you can't execute it. The effective charter school executive not only knows how to write a plan (*Step Four: Write Out*), but even more crucially, how to *carry out* a plan.

In what sounds like a contradiction, strategic planning at this stage actually ceases to be primarily a planning process. The nature of the task is now almost entirely operational. But while emphasizing the operational nature of carrying out the plan, I also want to highlight something that Ram Charan and Larry Bossidy say in their book, *Execution: The Discipline of Getting Things Done*. Namely, strategic planning is an iterative process, i.e., the plan is always morphing in response to the environment, so you're never really done planning.

Other than decisions that involve extraordinary commitments, such as purchasing a new piece of property, or building a new facility, the day-to-day operation of the school is, or should be, entirely under the direction of the school's executive. As I am fond of saying, the role of management is to *execute* (the plan); the role of the board is to *ensure* (that the results are satisfactorily achieved). Whenever the board strays over the line and begins carrying out the plan, it is entangling itself in the job of management. The board may think that it is trying to help, but helping outside one's area of expertise usually produces what I call "half-for-the-price-of-two results,"—a descriptor I invented by observing my two daughters. When they were young, they used to "help" my wife make cookies. Their help resulted in a job that took twice as long to complete, created twice the mess to clean up, but produced cookies that were only half as good. (But, yes, I still smiled and said, "Mmm, these are delicious!") So consider yourself forewarned: Board "help" in operations usually produces "half-for-the-price-of-two results." (For board members that find involvement in school operations irresistible, my advice is to obtain the necessary credentials and get a school to hire you.)

The job of executing a plan is not necessarily difficult, but it is laden with details. There are dozens, sometimes hundreds, of details that must be concurrently addressed in running a school. And the bigger the school, the more the details.

Of course, the job of the executive isn't so much one of actually carrying out those details as it is one of getting his or her team to execute them. This means the executive must be a master at delegating, an extensive discussion of which is beyond the scope of this book. But let us highlight a few key elements of carrying out a strategic plan.

First, because other people will be involved in carrying out any plan, the executive has to divide responsibilities among a team. In larger schools, the executive may have the advantage of having a team of several principals or other organizationally subordinate administrators. In smaller schools, lead teachers or others with partial management responsibilities may comprise the team.

The executive should meet with this team frequently to review the school's progress *against the plan*. In addition to meeting weekly, which is common, I recommend an offsite quarterly review in which the principals, directors, assistants, and so on each present a one- or two-page written summary of how their department or area of responsibility is performing against the plan. The key to making such meetings effective is to keep the focus on outcomes. At the beginning of each meeting, it is useful to reread the board's stated objectives, plus those the executive has added. Ask people to *rigorously evaluate how well* the school is doing against those goals.

A word of caution: It's very easy to be drawn into long process discussions that end up going nowhere. The executive who knows how to carry out a plan does not allow the team to be drawn into such discussions. If such discussions *are* necessary—and they occasionally are—they should never be mistaken by the executive as having the same value as a discussion focused on *achieving the outcomes*. Process discussions are only valuable to the extent that they get the school to the right outcome.

Second, the executive must ensure that he or she is delegating sufficient authority necessary to get the job done. The goal is to cultivate leaders who think for themselves. An organization full of people continuously asking permission to do their jobs will not be a high-performing one. This doesn't mean that people are free to operate outside parameters, such as budget, but the parameters should be clearly articulated so that people can operate within them without having to constantly circle back for permission. If your direct reports are frequently asking for approval to do their job, you're not doing yours.

Third, you must reward your top performers. The idea of incentives or rewards to accomplish great things in a charter school is not a radical proposition. Even a cursory understanding of human nature tells us that if you want more of something, you reward it. If you want less of something, you punish or ignore it. You're free, of course, to run your school across the grain of human nature, but you'll get better results more consistently when you reciprocate some of the value produced by your top performers.

Fourth, the executive must be willing to hold direct reports accountable for failing to achieve stated outcomes. While it is always difficult to remove people from the school, the executive who shrinks from this responsibility is not exercising leadership. I'm not saying that you have to be heavy-handed in your treatment of subordinates, but if you don't replace low achievers—despite whatever political blowback comes your way—then you're allowing the organization to be limited.

Lastly, I believe in the value of periodically celebrating the team's achievements. Again, this goes to human nature. People have a need for closure (to which the school year automatically and conveniently lends itself) and a need to bask in what they've accomplished. Even at home when you cut the grass, trim the shrubs, and rake the debris, it's nice to sit on the deck that evening and enjoy the results of your work.

By the way, don't confuse holding celebrations with the kids as being sufficient. Your team needs to periodically (once or twice a year) celebrate in a way that focuses on what they've accomplished. Such celebrations are part of the overall culture that you want to build. They communicate to people that what they do matters. And the need to hear that message from others doesn't end when we graduate from high school or college.

Using the 80/20 Principle to Carry Out the Strategic Plan

As a charter school executive, there are hundreds of details clamoring for your attention. This reality of school leadership is especially evident in smaller charter schools (150 to 250 students), where there is no one to share the executive leadership load. How does one successfully execute the plan while attending to all the details? You don't.

Instead of doing tasks simply because they present themselves, I recommend that charter school executives apply the 80/20 principle. In so doing, you discover that your involvement in only 20 percent of those details will generate a significantly disproportionate value to the school. The opposite is also true: 80 percent of things that you respond to or become involved in produce very little benefit (the trivial many), *relative to the vital few that you should use your time for*. It is important to recognize that it is not that a particular activity is inherently low value—*it's you being the one to do it as the executive that makes it low value*.

The key to dramatically increasing your effectiveness begins by analyzing what you spend your time doing. Start by separating your tasks into high and low categories. Once you've analyzed the results, you can, as Timothy Ferriss says in his excellent book, *The 4-Hour Work Week*, delegate, outsource, batch, or simply stop doing most of the low-value tasks. The resulting time that you free up can be used for high-value tasks, such as producing high student achievement. And since high-value tasks produce a disproportionate return, you will have exponentially increased your effectiveness.

For school executives, this naturally leads to the question, "What are my high-value and low-value tasks?"

The answer I'm going to give should be used only as a general rule of thumb because, in part, high value and low value depend on what you're exceptionally good at doing and how much help you have as an executive. For example, if you lead a school of 1,000 students, one set of your primary high-value tasks will be hiring, coaching, developing, and renewing the principals that report to you. If, on the other hand, you lead a school of 175, your high-value tasks will be hiring, coaching, developing, and renewing the faculty. Another example: An executive in a school of 1,000 students would not spend time doing teacher evaluations, whereas the same task would be a high-value task for an executive in a school of 175.

One aspect of leveraging the 80/20 principle, as guru Richard Koch notes in his many excellent books, is to discontinue doing most things that you're only modestly good at because they chew up time that could be used for things you are exceptionally good at. You will create disproportionate value for the school by focusing only on those things you are exceptionally good at. In fact, you will dramatically revolutionize your leadership once you fully apply the 80/20 principle to your work.

But understand that the above description is only a generalization. This means that you may still have to forgo something you're exceptionally good at doing if that task takes you away from accomplishing the board's goals. For example, you may be an extraordinary classroom teacher, but as a school executive you cannot afford to spend much of your time (if any) teaching and expect that you'll still have the time and energy to lead the school to superior performance.

A fundamental truth of being a successful executive is recognizing that the nature of your job is different than when you were in the classroom. Some people who have been ultra-successful in the classroom fail to achieve superior performance as executives because they don't understand that at each level of school leadership, the "20 percenters" change. Specifically, how you allocate your time, the tasks you do, and the sense of accomplishment you receive from doing them change when you move from the classroom to the administrative office. For further reading on this, I recommend a book by Ram Charan, Stephen Drotter, and James Noel entitled *The Leadership Pipeline*.

Figure 4 proposes a general separation of high- and low-value school operational tasks you can use to stimulate your thinking. I've done my best not to present any imaginary tasks. Everything on the list is something I've done as a school executive at one time or another. Feel free to add your own examples.

Astute observers may instantly notice that the ratio of low-value to high-value tasks in Figure 4 is about four to one. This ratio illustrates the 80/20 principle almost perfectly. To get the maximum benefit from the figure, set aside an afternoon to reflect on the tasks, then think about what your next work week will look like if you did only high-value tasks.

High-Value Tasks

Thinking
Attending weekly civic club meetings
Preparing for board meetings
Observing classroom instruction*
Coaching direct reports
Interviewing/selecting staff*
Strategic planning
Preparing for accreditation
Spending time in the hallways

Reviewing lesson plans*
Analyzing test data to inform
  instruction
Visiting other high performing schools
Planning your weekly/monthly
  schedule
Conducting faculty renewal/
  development*
Developing your authorizer relationship

Low-Value Tasks

Administering tests
Answering your telephone
  (unscreened calls)
Approving lunch menus
Assembling handbooks
Attending too many sporting events
Building/maintaining your website
Buying classroom supplies
Changing light bulbs
Checking email multiple times a day
Classroom teaching
Cleaning the faculty lounge
Coaching sports or clubs
Collecting water samples
  (from well systems)
Conducting fire drills
Counseling students
Creating class schedules
Creating restroom usage schedules
Cutting the grass
Designing office forms
Designing the Yellow Page ad
Developing the budget
Directing drop-off and pick-up
Drafting memos
Driving the bus
Enforcing dress codes
Entering data into the database
Faxing documents
Filing
Filling out compliance paperwork
Fundraising
Going on field trips
Helping office staff assemble
  direct mailings
Inventorying books

Laying out the annual report
Leading assemblies
Mopping the floor
Moving classroom furniture
Operating a backhoe
Painting classrooms
Pressure washing sidewalks
Reconciling the school's checking
  account
Refereeing basketball
Resolving routine discipline
  problems
Reviewing asbestos inspector
  credentials
Searching lockers
Shelving library books
Signing checks
Soliciting bids to repair the
  playground fence
Substituting
Supervising septic system
  installation
Talking to salespeople
Teaching staff how to use office
  software
Too many meetings with
  faculty/staff
Too many meetings with individual
  families
Troubleshooting computer problems
Un-jamming the copier
Unstopping clogged toilets
Writing faculty/staff handbooks
Writing parent/student handbooks
Writing the school newsletter

*Items followed by an asterisk are only high value for executives without a
management team

FIGURE 4. *Comparison of Low-Value and High-Value Charter School Executive Tasks*

"Show Me the Money—Maybe"

I've met some school leaders who eschew the idea of incentives because, in the words of one such person, they view "getting to keep one's job as *the* reward."

My response is that mediocre performers are the only people who view keeping their jobs as a reward. In contrast, top performers (usually, no surprise here, about 20 percent of the people in an organization unless you've intentionally staffed the school to counter this phenomenon) know that they can create new opportunities for themselves if they need or want to. Rewarding and expanding this group is always an executive's best strategy for building an organization.

Rewards don't necessarily have to be cash. In fact, if you give everyone the same reward, you will have defeated the purpose of having incentives. As Ram Charan and Larry Bossidy note in their *New York Times* bestselling *Execution: The Discipline of Getting Things Done*, you must differentiate rewards according to the individual and according to his or her performance. You must do this, partly because the employee must regard the reward as such in his or her own mind. Thus, for example, a person whose spouse earns $350,000 a year may not regard a cash bonus of $750 as much of a reward (in the sense that it may not influence the individual's future actions). Instead, a paid sabbatical or some other reward *tailored* to the individual must be selected, assuming his or her performance warrants it.

Step Six: Measure Out

At this stage of the strategic planning process, the board must again assume a lead role, though it is likely the executive or some other professional with pertinent expertise will have to guide it through the evaluation process the first few times. In this step, the board measures the progress of the school against the outcomes it determined in *Step One: Figure Out.* In so doing, besides capitalizing on the observation that in organizations, "What gets measured gets done," the board is actually fulfilling its governance obligations to the taxpayers by ensuring that the school accomplishes its purposes. *The process of ensuring is the very essence of board governance.* (Note: Though sometimes attributed to Peter Drucker or Tom Peters, the axiom, "What gets measured gets done," was attributed *by* Tom Peters in his book, *In Search of Excellence,* to Mason Haire.)

The evaluation process can seem overwhelming if you don't know where to begin, so this chapter is divided into three parts. The first part is devoted to explaining *how* the board evaluates the school using one of three methods. Though it may seem counterintuitive to say that there are only three methods by which the board can evaluate the executive, these three are, in fact, the only ways you can do it.

In the second part of this chapter, I discuss *what* the board evaluates. You already know that the board establishes outcomes, not inputs or processes. *This section will tell you how to avoid four common pitfalls in the process of measuring the school's performance.* It also contains some insight on using qualitative evidence in combination with its more precise counterpart, quantitative measures.

In the third part, I synthesize these two sections into practical steps for conducting the evaluation process. If you've ever paid an outside consultant to help you evaluate your school executive, you might find that these steps alone were worth the price of this book.

Part One—How a Board Evaluates the School

First, it is imperative to understand that when the board evaluates its executive, it *is* evaluating the school and vice versa. This is because the executive is the one person who is accountable to the board for the performance of the school. For example, if the fourth-grade reading scores are in the tank, the board doesn't (or shouldn't) call the fourth-grade teacher to the table to give an account. It is the executive who must answer for the performance of the entire school. Thus, *when the board is evaluating the school, it is evaluating its executive.*

Among the many gems of wisdom contained in John Carver's masterful description of how boards can function effectively is a simple explanation of ways in which the board can evaluate how well the executive (which Carver refers to as the CEO) is fulfilling the board's stated outcomes. To develop a fuller understanding of how a board can evaluate its executive, I again encourage boards and executives to read his signature work, *Boards That Make a Difference.*

Although I have restated Carver's three ways of evaluating in my own words such that a board can use these methods apart from Policy Governance, fundamentally, as Carver has established, there are *only* three ways or methods by which the board may evaluate the executive. In no particular order, they are as follows:

1. The board can evaluate the school's performance by directly examining it for itself.
2. The board can evaluate the school's performance by requiring the executive to submit a self-evaluation or self-report.
3. The board can evaluate the school's performance with the help of an expert, such as a consultant or accountant, who is not a part of the board or employed in the school.

Any of these three can be combined with the others, which the board may need to do, depending on what is being evaluated. For example, executives often submit financial reports to their boards. Though these may not have actually been written by the executive, by submitting them to the board, he or she is essentially issuing a self-report (method #2).

In the case of charter schools, such a self-report by itself is insufficient because of the board's obligations to the taxpayers. Thus, an auditor should also be *selected by the board* to render an *independent opinion* (i.e., independent of management influence) through an annual audit (method # 3).

There is not, however, such a thing as a charter school being created to produce clean audit opinions, so this is not the kind of outcome the board creates in figuring out what it wants. To be sure, improper financial management has gotten *many* charter schools into hot water, but staying out of trouble is not the same as fulfilling your mission. *The purpose of the board is to ensure that both occur.* (For a complete discussion on creating policies that empower the board to maintain proper control over such things as finances, again, I refer the reader to John Carver. No finer conception of *how* the board fulfills such important roles exists.)

Thus, while the board has an obligation to ensure that the taxpayers' money is properly handled, the concern of this book is on outcomes in strategic planning. Let's apply the three methods above to the board's evaluation of the executive's progress against the stated outcomes for the school. The method the board chooses will depend, in part, on the outcome that is being measured.

For example, the board could examine for itself (method #1) what percentage of students achieved proficiency on the state test (an absolute performance measure). Although there are complex statistical computations involved in the design and scoring of state tests, generally the reporting is straightforward.

But what about more complex outcomes, such as the board's goal that every child in the school achieves a year's worth of growth for a year's worth of instruction (a student gains performance measure)? Although it could be reported to the board as the percentage of students that achieved the goal, value-added testing is based on a more complex statistical method. This implies that, at a minimum, the board is able to recognize when a legitimate value-added instrument (test) was used. For goals involving such complex measures, the board may want to retain an outside expert (method #3).

Then, what about method #2? Isn't it contradictory to utilize a report from the executive if the board is supposed to be doing the evaluation? No—provided that you carefully observe the following: When the executive writes a self-evaluation (i.e., a report in which he or she uses his or her own judgment about the performance of the organization), the board needs to require that the executive *demonstrate* the performance by substantiating it with evidence.

In other words, the self-evaluations from the executive don't say things like, "I'm pleased with the mission-specific achievements of our students." That doesn't demonstrate anything. Instead, it should say something like, "The board's mission-specific outcomes require that 'every graduate is conversationally fluent in Mandarin.' In the April standardized test of fluency in Mandarin, 89 percent of our students scored proficiently. The remaining 11 percent had skills one level below fluency."

You might be wondering, "Why would the board even use its executive to evaluate the school's performance?" The answer is practical: It's too expensive to retain an outside expert to evaluate every aspect of the school's performance. Besides which, outside expertise isn't really necessary for assessing some outcomes.

Again, the most essential points are that there are three methods by which the board may evaluate the school, and depending on that which is being evaluated, the board will use one or more of the methods. These methods constitute *how* the evaluation is conducted and they are used (in the context of strategic planning) only to compare stated outcomes to actual performance. In the next section, I expand on comparing stated outcomes to actual outcomes by describing some key differences in indicators.

Part Two—What the Board Evaluates

Thus far, we've established that the board evaluates the executive by evaluating the school's performance against prescribed outcomes. And you should recall at this point that those outcomes were determined by the board all the way back at *Step One*, during which the board figured out what the school was to accomplish.

From the moment the strategic planning process begins, then, both the board and its executive know what is going to be assessed. When this is clearly spelled out (even in an employment agreement or a management company contract), everyone benefits, not the least of whom are the kids you are serving.

It's worth emphasizing that *evaluating an executive against anything other than stated expectations is both unprofessional and unfair.* Unfair evaluations hurt people, damage the reputation of the school, and undermine the entire charter school sector. (See the sidebar: "I'm Thinking of Leaving Charter Schools.")

As I've also explained, sometimes there is technical prowess required to do the actual work of measuring the school's performance against the outcomes. For such situations, a qualified consultant can bring the necessary expertise to the table (in addition to objectivity).

Now let's talk about indicators and the evidence the board considers when it is evaluating the school's performance. Even if you hire a consultant to assist in your evaluation, understanding differences in key indicators and types of evidence will be extremely valuable. (You might even use the information below to gauge the appropriateness of a prospective consultant, as not all consultants are created equal.)

Two Types of Indicators, Two Types of Evidence

When it comes to indicators, there are two types the board can examine: 1) Indicators that point to the school's present performance and 2) indicators that point to the school's future performance (even if crudely). For the sake of simplicity, we'll just call these *present performance indicators* and *future performance indicators*. In some cases, a single indicator can be both: Like an azimuth on a map, it can indicate both your present position and the trajectory you're following (by which you can estimate when you will arrive at a future destination). Let's look at an analogy illustrating the difference, followed by specific examples of each.

Let's say that your favorite NFL team wins the Super Bowl. At the time they win, their victory is the ultimate (for a professional football team) present performance indicator. It's time to uncork the champagne and celebrate! As spectacular a feat as winning the Super Bowl is, however, it does not have much, if any, predictive power about the possibility of winning the Super Bowl in the future. The head coach or the owner cannot use last year's ultimate win as a future performance indicator for the current season. Only as the team begins playing in the new season do those wins represent a future performance indicator.

Present Performance Indicators

Present performance indicators have value because you can use them to assess whether the school has fulfilled its mission *up to the present* (defined as when the test was given). Generally, when the board looks at test scores, most of the time it is evaluating the school's present performance. (I try to avoid technical talk, but some readers will recognize that test scores from certain value-added instruments are both a present performance indicator and a future performance indicator because high correlation coefficients between some instruments and some state tests suggest future performance on the latter.) For example, if the board examines state test data that show 83 percent of kids achieved proficiency in writing, the data are functioning as a present performance indicator. Other examples of present performance indicators include (but are not limited to):

- Percentage of kids who take (and pass) Advanced Placement exams
- Percentage of kids who graduate on time
- Total college scholarships awarded (for academic or athletic achievement)
- Number of National Merit Exam semi-finalists and finalists
- Percentage of kids who enroll in college
- Percentage of kids who graduate from college
- Percentage of kids who place in science fairs
- Percentage of kids who read "x" number of books during the year
- Percentage of kids who achieve a year's worth of gains in a year's time
- The school's performance relative to other schools on state tests
- Percentage of kids who can proficiently repair a small engine
- Percentage of kids who successfully complete their probation and enter society as contributing members
- Percentage of kids who are conversationally fluent in Mandarin

Can you figure out which of the above present performance indicators apply to the four categories of outcomes discussed in *Step One: Figure Out*? Can you think of present performance indicators that you would add to the list for your school?

Future Performance Indicators

In contrast to present performance indicators, however, *future performance indicators are valuable because they always point toward the future accomplishment of the organization.* And since a charter school, like all other organizations, does not have the luxury of resting on its laurels, the board should be obsessed with achieving future success. The challenge with future performance indicators, however, is that because they require a predictive interpretation, they tend to be less precise and less reliable than present performance indicators. Nevertheless, here are some examples of future performance indicators:

- Percentage of students indicating they plan to attend college when they graduate (but haven't yet actually enrolled)
- Percentage of students who enroll in Advanced Placement courses
- Relative performance data consistently trending upward
- Gains testing data
- Percentage of students actively fulfilling the terms of their probation (e.g., attending school, staying clean, following curfews, etc.)
- Increasing library usage (apart from class requirements)
- Favorable site visit results or reviews (of academic performance) from authorizer
- High daily attendance or trending upward (in cases where it has been low)
- Discipline problems low or trending downward (in cases where they have been high)
- Percentage of students involved in academic extracurricular activities (e.g., chess club, book club, foreign language club, art club, music club, etc.)

As with present performance indicators, can you figure out (without looking back at *Step One: Figure Out*), in which category of student outcomes the items from the list above belong? What future performance indicators would you add to your school?

Indicators That Are Both Present and Future Performance

The fact that more than 80 percent of KIPP kids enroll in college is both a present performance indicator and a future performance indicator that the school is achieving its mission because a high percentage of disadvantaged minorities (especially in urban areas) are going to college. As a future performance indicator, some percentage of these students will graduate from college. (Obviously, in terms of ultimate success, we don't just want kids to go to college—we want them to graduate.)

Two Types of Evidence

As mentioned in *Step One: Figure Out*, there are two possible ways to measure outcomes. One way is quantitatively—using numbers—which is how most paper-and-pencil tests are measured. By acknowledging that such tests have weaknesses (as I have and do), I am in no way saying they are useless. The board needs quantitative measures to be able to assess the school's performance.

But quantitative isn't everything. After all, as examples in this book illustrate, there are things that are better measured qualitatively. Instead of using numbers to describe performance, qualitative measures rely on other kinds of evidence to demonstrate performance. For example, a student portfolio of projects might reflect achievement.

Quantitative and qualitative evidence can be used to assess either type of indicator—present performance or future performance. What follows are four pitfalls the board needs to avoid when conducting school evaluations.

Avoiding Evaluation Pitfalls

1. Avoid Using Present or Future Performance Indicators to the Exclusion of the Other.

There is a danger in relying on only one type of indicator *when you need to evaluate both the present performance of the school and the future trajectory it is on.* Looking only at present performance indicators can cause the board to either be short-sighted about what might be accomplished in the future or to think that its present successes guarantee future successes. On the other hand, looking only at future performance indicators may cause the board to lose sight of how well the school is performing in the here and now. Rather than rely on one type of indicator, the board should compile as much evidence of success as it can, evaluating both types of indicators.

2. Avoid Using Only Quantitative Measures

Second, both present performance indicators and future performance indicators that are qualitative tend to be less precise than those that are quantitative, creating a tendency to avoid using them. I think this is because we've been conditioned to accept *only* precise measures of performance for schools. This is an enormous mistake because qualitative evidence can provide insight on the school's performance that quantitative information is simply incapable of giving.

For example, think about a charter school that exists so that kids attain high achievement in the performing arts. What might the board look at in terms of performance indicators (either present or future)? It's safe to say, probably not tests that generate quantitative results.

For the sake of discussion, let's assume that in such a school, there are students who compose music. While difficult to measure quantitatively, composing one's own music might be considered a crude qualitative indicator of achievement. Some professional judgment on the part of the faculty (and perhaps qualified others) would likely be rendered as to the quality of such compositions. Their judgment, in turn, would be summarized and reported to the board (through the executive), who in turn would evaluate the report to determine whether the achievement of the students satisfies the outcomes prescribed by the board.

You noticed, of course, that no quantitative measures were involved. Thus, even if the evidence for performance is qualitative and imprecise, it's perfectly reasonable, even preferable, to use it as needed.

This is a good place to re-emphasize that *all measures are imperfect.* There is no such thing as *the* single best measure of school performance. We want all kids to achieve a minimum level of proficiency in language, math, science, history, and the arts, but superior school performance goes way beyond simply measuring minimal levels of proficiency in core academic subjects.

Truly amazing schools potentiate students in becoming painters, sculptors, software programmers, inventors, authors, photographers, dancers, musicians, scientists, thinkers, philosophers, mechanics, robotics engineers, designers, poets, tacticians, and leaders. (For every example listed, I can point to actual charter schools where performance indicators demonstrate that students are actually becoming these things.) Achievement in these various disciplines can be measured in a variety of ways, few of which involve traditional paper-and-pencil tests generating quantitative results.

3. Avoid the Most Common Error

There is a common mistake in evaluating the school that the board needs to avoid. Rather than name it directly, however, look at the bullet list below and see if you can find what *all* the measures have in common (hint: They are things on which the board should not evaluate the school. Can you figure out why?):

- Of teachers newly hired, 83 percent have advanced degrees
- New curriculum purchased this year
- Five hundred new books added to the library
- New assessment program being implemented
- High-caliber teacher development program being implemented
- Enrollment increased (apart from evidence showing it is being driven by academic achievement)

- Reduction in student-to-teacher ratio
- More rigorous classroom teacher evaluation being implemented
- Everyone is dedicated and working hard

Give yourself an "A" if you recognized that *everything in the list is an input, not an outcome*. This is a critical distinction the board needs to make because **there is an almost natural temptation to assess progress on outcomes by measuring or examining inputs!**

Here's an illustration to make the point that measuring inputs is the wrong focus. Imagine you're part of a bluegrass band. You and the other members of the band have music degrees, practice a lot, love making audiences happy, have quality instruments, work together well, spend time studying bluegrass music, and so on. What do these things indicate about the quality of the band's music? Nothing.

Granted, all of those things *are* necessary inputs, *but measuring them is not the same thing as measuring outcomes*.

Instead of trying to measure the band's success on inputs, we would do much better to look at the number of albums sold (quantitative measure of quality based on the judgment of consumers), the number of gigs booked (same), the reaction of audiences to its live performances (qualitative measure), and favorable media mentions (possibly a future performance indicator of success if the articles are trending favorably on the assumption that the better the band is, the more favorable media coverage it will receive), and so on.

I want to be clear: The right inputs are absolutely essential. That's the key reason I urge you to visit other schools in *Step Two: Find Out*. You need to look at what kinds of inputs world-class schools use so that you can use the same or similar inputs.

To recap *the vital few* in terms of key inputs, a school needs *the most qualified people* it can hire and retain. It needs to develop, reward, and renew its top performers. There is also no question that a school needs the best curriculum it can buy or create, appropriate to the school's unique purpose. We've also talked about the critical variable of retaining the right school executive who will, in fact, draw on his or her expertise to assemble the right inputs. The mere fact that he or she does so, however, is no indicator of success, present or future.

To confirm this, think back to the NFL example. If you owned the team, although you'd want as many top players in the country on your roster as you can afford, simply having them on the team doesn't indicate one way or another that you're going to have a winning season (though I'd definitely rather take my chances with them than without).

4. Avoid Measuring Only Things Easily Assessed

A fourth pitfall to be avoided is failing to evaluate an outcome because it is hard to measure or assess, or even worse, not prescribing an outcome to be achieved because it is not easily measured or assessed (not to be confused with things like self-esteem improvement goals that are neither measurable nor on which school performance can be assessed.)

Here again, as in *Step One: Figure Out*, I encourage the board to gather *both* quantitative and qualitative data, as needed. As previously described, qualitative data can, and probably will, be less precise than quantitative data. But, to modify Carver a bit, it is better to use an imprecise measure (qualitative) of the right thing than to use an exact measure (quantitative) of the wrong thing. Let's consider an example of a student outcome where a qualitative, but imprecise, measure produces useful evaluation evidence.

Suppose the board establishes the following outcome: "Graduates will know how to use their artistic talents to create wealth for themselves." Obviously, a goal like this does not lend itself to quantitative measures, such as traditional paper-and-pencil tests, *but that doesn't make it any less worthy of a goal.*

So how might the board assess this outcome? Perhaps, the executive might direct the art teacher to work with the students in arranging several exhibitions throughout the year in which students will have the opportunity to sell their work from a portfolio they assemble.

After selling their work, the teacher might assign students to write papers on what they learned about using their talents to create wealth (sales) for themselves. The teacher would probably be looking for insights such as "Items less than $5 sold better than more expensive items" or "I was able to increase my sales in the second exhibition by setting up an easel on which I worked while people talked to me about my art."

Following several exhibitions, the teacher might assemble the students into groups with instructions to synthesize the lessons from all the papers (anonymously). The results produced by each group could then be compiled into a class pamphlet on creating wealth through art which the students could publish and sell on the Internet. (As you know, there is no learning experience quite as valuable as when a student teaches something to another.)

At the conclusion of the year, or some other interval, the board could direct the executive to submit a self-report in which he or she guides the board in evaluating the results. The board then uses the evidence demonstrated in the report to assess how well its outcome was achieved.

You should notice something about all the steps I just described. They do not require the students to make a lot of money, or for the pamphlet to sell well. The board's objective is qualitatively measured through the work and insights produced by the students.

> Quantitative? No
> Imprecise? Yes.
> Valuable? Extremely.

Part Three—Practical Steps the Board Can Take in Conducting the Evaluation

Everything I've written in this book up to this point is intended to lay the foundation for the school evaluation process. *It is vitally important that your board does not attempt to use the following steps without reading and understanding that framework.*

As you begin the process, the thing to keep foremost in the minds of board members is that evaluating the school's performance is identical to evaluating the school executive's performance because he or she is *the one person* directly accountable to the board for producing it. Throughout this book, I have used school and executive performance interchangeably and will do so again in this section. Thus, whenever I write that the board evaluates its executive by examining such and such an indicator, you should interpret that to mean the same thing as the board evaluates the school by examining the same indicator in the same way. Before proceeding through these steps, be certain your board is absolutely clear on this point.

Evaluation Steps

1. I recommend that the board form a committee that will take the lead in guiding the evaluation process. To accomplish this, the board directs the committee to ensure that the process adheres to the integrity of *The Seven Outs*. **If the board has deviated from the principles described in *The Seven Outs*, please do not use these steps, nor refer to your evaluation as having followed these steps.**

2. The board needs to establish a date range during which it wants to conduct the evaluation process. This range should generally run about three months prior to the time the board wants the process to be completed. This allows plenty of time to gather the data and evidence the board will need to conduct the evaluation. *If the board will be making the executive's contract renewal decision based on the evaluation, it is of critical importance that the board complete its evaluation by the end of January, **at the latest**.* This is a simple courtesy to the executive who will likely, at a minimum, need all of February, March, April, and possibly May, in which to find another school. (As pointed out in the Breezy Palms Charter School story, because of the cyclical nature of the American school year, there is generally a small window of time in which a school executive can find another position.) Notifying him or her as early

as possible also maximizes the board's window to conduct its own search for a new executive.

3. Once the date range has been set, set aside some time for the board and executive to review the board's stated outcomes for the school. You will recall that apart from the four to six stated outcomes (the school's vital few), the board has nothing against which to evaluate its executive. Thus, the review process sharpens everyone's focus for the work that is about to begin.

4. Review the following three concepts and decide which combination you need to evaluate the school's performance against the board's four to six stated outcomes:

    a. The three evaluation methods presented in the first part of this chapter (inspection by the board, executive self-report, and outside expert)

    b. The two types of indicators presented in the second part of this chapter (present performance and future performance)

    c. The two types of evidence the board can examine in evaluating the school (quantitative and qualitative)

    For any outcome being evaluated, you need at least one element from each category, i.e., one method + one indicator + one type of evidence. Example: The board has a stated outcome that at least 90 percent of third through eighth-grade students who have been enrolled for at least a school year prior to the state test will achieve proficiency in math and English language arts. In discussing how this performance is best evaluated, the board might logically decide to accept a self-report from the executive, in which the board acknowledges that it will look at the current results (a present performance indicator) and that the data will be quantitative, but reported qualitatively (i.e., basic, proficient, advanced, etc.).

5. Evaluate each of the four to six outcomes *in writing*. Gather as much data and evidence for each outcome as you can.

6. Review the written evaluation with the executive, usually in closed session. (However, check with the board's attorney to find out the specifics of your state's open meeting or sunshine laws).

7. Allow the executive to respond in writing to any elements of the evaluation with which he or she disagrees. As a board, decide how to respond to any such disagreement.

8. If the executive's performance merits an incentive, award it.

We've Done the Evaluation: What's Next?

You may be thinking, what does our board do if some of its outcomes were achieved, but not as well as we hoped? Do we have to fire our executive? The answer, of course is, no, you don't have to fire your executive. The board simply has to use its judgment to determine whether the actual performance against the stated outcomes is acceptable.

Keep in mind that the perfect executive hasn't yet been invented. So the board's standard should never be perfection. The board simply needs to make a reasonable evaluation of the outcomes. The most reliable performance evaluation occurs with trend data. For example, if the percentage of kids achieving a year's worth of gains is less than 100 percent, is this year's percentage higher than last year's? In other words, is it trending in the right direction? If it is trending in the right direction, what's the rate of increase? At the present rate, will the school hit its objective in three years or fifteen?

Does this result in an element of subjectivity? Yes, but almost all evaluations do. But one of the advantages presented in *The Seven Outs* is that subjectivity is significantly narrowed to stated outcomes. A key difference posited in this book is that the board is saying which outcomes it wants *in advance of evaluating its school's performance.* That's light years ahead of how most charter schools are evaluating their executive, if they are evaluating him or her at all. Once that evaluation is complete, the board is ready to share the school's accomplishments with the world. It's time to shout out the school's accomplishments.

"I'm Thinking of Leaving Charter Schools."

A young charter school executive approached me after a conference workshop a couple of years ago, distraught that she had just
received an email informing her that she was fired. She said she had
received no formal evaluation or any advance notice that her job
was in jeopardy. The board apparently waited for her to attend the
conference, then held a meeting without her knowledge in which
they fired her. (Of course, I had no knowledge of her actual performance, but clearly the evaluation process itself was unfair.)

Unfortunately, as I explained to her, there are dysfunctional
boards that have no sense of professional (or even personal) pro-
priety. Sometimes they will trash their executive without remorse
just because one or two board members simply don't like him or
her. And as in the case of this young lady, no formal evaluation
ever takes place. (A consultant friend of mine wryly refers to this
as the executive receiving his or her first evaluation on a piece of
pink paper.)

The most tragic element of the episode was reflected in her
lament that due to the unfairness of the situation, she was thinking
about leaving the charter sector. There in front of me was an articu-
late, energetic young person with an earned doctorate, willing to
work in a difficult start-up school—and *she was thinking of leaving
the sector altogether*. I wondered to myself, "Isn't this the very kind
of leader that organizations such as *New Leaders for New Schools*
are feverishly working to produce? And here a board tossed this
one aside like an empty milk carton. What a shame."

I urge you to do all in your power to prevent your board from
ever acting with such callous disregard for others. Evaluate fairly
and formally. If you need to replace your executive, treat him or

her in a manner that is just (i.e., no secret meetings and personal grudges) and dignified (i.e., no email notifications).

If not for the executive's sake, then be professional for your school's sake. The kind of seasoned candidates you'd want to build a world-class school that the board will interview next will be keenly interested in knowing how the board handled the separation of the previous executive. If you voted him or her off the island unfairly, be assured that the backsplash will eventually be on you.

Step Seven: Shout Out

In this final step, the board and the executive work together to disseminate the school's accomplishments. I call this step shout-out as a salute to Achievement First, a high-performing charter organization, as previously mentioned. It publishes school accomplishments in *Shout Out!*, a tri-annual newsletter. Like Achievement First, you will want to shout-out your school's accomplishments.

A simple reality in today's world constitutes the premise of this seventh step in strategic planning: It is insufficient to achieve world-class results; *you also have to broadcast them.* Your school's parents, teachers, students, authorizer, state association, local media, and broader community are among the stakeholders that *need to know* what the school is accomplishing.

Granted, your school might not ever get primetime television coverage like KIPP Academy and High Tech High, but you don't need to appear on *Oprah* or *60 Minutes* to be effective in getting the word out. There are many low-cost things you can do to inform people about your school's accomplishments.

Although it is beyond the scope of this book, creating a media plan that describes how the school will shout out its extraordinary accomplishments can greatly benefit any charter school. Reporting gives your school

147

visibility and credibility, which can translate into much-needed community support. A good plan would incorporate a wide range of media exposure strategies, from developing earned media (i.e., news coverage) to paying for advertising.

Even in the absence of a full-fledged media plan, however, your school needs to spread the word of its successes. Consistently doing so creates a wide base of supporters that every school needs. To get you started on thinking about the seventh step, I've listed three ways your school can inform others about all that it is accomplishing.

The Traditional Publishing Venue

Desktop publishing has revolutionized the print industry to the point where printing costs are insignificant. Thus, publishing your accomplishments through print media is at the top of this list because it's one of the most cost-effective strategies, considering how many people you can reach relative to cost. (At the risk of sounding like I'm telling one of those "we walked to school in the snow without shoes" stories, I remember my first year as a school executive, 1990. We rewrote the parent/student handbook and had it professionally printed and saddle-stitched with a cardstock cover. To the best of my recollection, the cost was about $4,000 for a few hundred copies. Mercifully, those days are behind us.)

Your charter school can have multiple print forums through which you can and should constantly sound the drumbeat of student achievements. These forums can include a newsletter or school newspaper, school calendars, letters, and—one of my favorites—the annual report. The latter has such potentially significant value that I want to devote a few paragraphs exclusively to discussing it.

First, your school actually needs accomplishments. If you don't have anything of substance to say, don't write one. But assuming that there is substance to the school's performance, the cost of such a report is minimized by its value. You should distribute this report far and wide in order to maximize its impact. Here are a few suggestions:

- Distribute the report to every existing family in the school. Many families may not read it, but simply receiving a high-quality report should help reinforce their decision that your school is right for their child. (In my experience, most families will at least look at the photos for their own children. In turn, they will show the report to other people, something which helps increase the school's visibility.)

- Include the most current year's edition with any literature you give to prospective families.

- Use the report as part of a targeted direct mail campaign (for example, a ZIP code or neighborhood in which school-aged kids served by your school happen to live).

- Put the report in the hands of community foundation directors to increase your chances of getting a sliver of local grant funding. (But be forewarned, these dollars are scarce and there's a lot of competition for them. Don't base your operating budget on them.)

- Take your authorizer to lunch and give him or her a copy. Considering how widely overlooked annual reports by charter schools are, most will be impressed that your school is on top of things (assuming again that you actually have meaningful results about which to boast—otherwise it's just another empty piece of advertising irrespective of the cover stock).

- If you have a relationship with the local newspaper, give a copy to the education reporter. "Local Charter School Makes Hometown Proud" stories always produce favorable benefits.

Brian's Quick Seminar on Producing Annual Reports

1. Budget for at least a two-color report. In the present media age, anything short of that is viewed by readers as dull.

2. I maintain a journal devoted exclusively to organizational accomplishments throughout the year. Once I'm ready to begin writing, all the high points are at my fingertips. This cuts research time down to almost nothing.

3. Photos and names—include lots of them. Be sure to include lots of photos and names. Few things have as much meaning to your readers as photos and names. (There, I made the point three times. Other than including lots of photos and names, you should be able to remember the key element of the annual report.) As far as collecting photos, direct your yearbook committee to supply you with a digital file of all photos taken throughout the year. These will probably be numerous enough that you won't have any difficulty coming up with imaginative shots. Oh, and did I mention to includes lots of photos and names?

4. Make sure every name is spelled correctly. If this requires getting the thing proofread and initialed by every teacher in the school, then do it. (Most people are irritated when their names are misspelled, especially when they feel they belong to a community such as your school. I still remember the fallout from an annual report years ago, in which a student's name was misspelled. I'll let you infer the error by simply telling you that the correct spelling was Skittel.)

5. Be careful not to contradict your core message of academic excellance with silly mistakes. (For the two people who are wondering, yes, I intentionally misspelled excellence to make my point.)

6. Hire a graphic artist to do the design and layout work. (For great prices on outsourcing, check out sites like www.elance. com. You'll be amazed at how cheaply and efficiently things can be outsourced.)

7. Be sure to print enough to keep at least a half-dozen extra file copies each year to maintain for the school's archives. Fifty years from now, if your charter school is still a world-class organization, people are going to enjoy looking at these relics from early years.

The Virtual Publishing Venue

Shout out your achievements—virtually. And talk about cheap! Websites and electronic newsletters can be full color, reach a potentially unlimited number of readers, include multi-media (podcast interviews, PDF downloads of your annual report, video-streaming) without incurring postage and printing costs. Why wouldn't you leverage the virtual realm? (Again, the technical part of this can be outsourced cheaply.)

Turn Your School-Wide Meetings into Student Exhibitions

Parents will come to events at school if it's to see their children exhibit their talents (as opposed to coming to hear the executive, board chair, or parent teacher president drone on in front of a microphone). My advice? Put the microphone in the closet and keep everyone off the stage except for the kids. But there's something even better than the stage.

Consider the benefit of demonstrating student achievement by having two school-wide meetings per year in which the kids display all kinds of work including publications, science projects, history projects, graphic arts, and so on. Such exhibitions have value because they involve the parents, bring the school community together, and give kids the opportunity to experience the pride of a job well done.

I attended one such exhibition on a spring evening on the Pt. Loma campus of High Tech High. The parents practically mobbed the place to see what their *high-school-age kids* had done. And while you might not think that high school kids like to show off their work, these kids were justifiably proud of their accomplishments. From the perspective of reporting out the school's accomplishments, I cannot imagine that a single parent left the event disappointed in what his or her children were learning.

Like so many other things the High Tech High folks have leveraged for their purpose, these project demonstration nights are a stroke of genius. These nights do so much to build confidence in the students, get families involved with their kids' education, and help create a sense of shared community. *Project exhibitions demonstrate the fulfillment of the school's mission like few things can.*

In closing, remember to keep your message simple and on point. By frequently repeating the board's four to six outcomes for the school, everyone stays unified around the school's core purposes. By combining print media, virtual media, and project exhibitions, your charter school can make huge strides at informing stakeholders just how much it is accomplishing. Use your imagination and creativity to combine the methods above to shout out your progress.

Epilogue:
The *Eighth Out*

One of the perks of working alongside witty people is that they keep you laughing. One such colleague, whom I mentioned in the acknowledgments' section of this book, is Amy Van Atten. Her deadpan sense of humor is, like certain types of software, always operating in the background. Thus, when I initially described *The Seven Outs* to her, she quipped, in less than a nanosecond, "You need to add an eighth out."

"What's that?" I asked, walking straight into her trap.

"If a charter school board can't do the first seven, they should *get out.*"

Although I laughed uproariously, I concur with Amy's point: If a board or CEO can't get the job done, it should step aside and make room for those who can. The reason is that good governance and strategic planning have high-stakes consequences riding on them, not the least of which is the preparedness of children for their *own future*. (Notice that I framed this sentence as an outcome rather than a process.)

And, when you consider that charter schools serve a high percentage of disadvantaged minority students (i.e., disproportionately higher than regular public schools), ensuring that they graduate your school with a sound education in hand is a matter of social justice. So a board that fails to properly govern and plan, resulting in a school where the kids are not learning as they should, is actually perpetuating social injustice.

Granted, the board may do so unwittingly because it doesn't know any better, or its members are caught up in roles in which they can act out their own personal dramas, or it has abdicated its responsibility for some other reason. But the consequences of the offense are nonetheless real: kids who either fail to graduate or graduate with a deplorable lack of skills, i.e., they can't read proficiently or perform basic math. Thus, they cannot think for themselves.

This is outrageously expensive, both in terms of lost human potential and the decline in national life. In other words, individual students suffer because they lack the skills that would make them economically class-mobile, and the nation suffers because its citizens are incapable of fulfilling their civic obligations because they lack even a working knowledge of economics, history, and government. If you've visited developing countries, you've witnessed the long term results of coupling economic deprivation with civic ignorance.

Charter schools were created to address these deficits. But the only way they can rise to meet the challenge is for boards to fully embrace their responsibilities. In addition to asking themselves the kinds of questions presented in this book, along with evaluating results produced in the schools they oversee, boards need to take seriously the challenge of developing their capacity. They can do this by studying books like this one, and by regularly evaluating their own effectiveness.

In closing, I hope you've enjoyed reading *The Seven Outs: Strategic Planning Made Easy for Charter Schools,* but more than that, I hope your board will apply its lessons to your school. When it does, you'll be thrusting the school forward in pursuit of great things as its students discover how exciting it is to live life fully potentiated.

References

Bossidy, L., and R. Charan. 2002. *Execution: The discipline of getting things done.* New York: Crown Business.

Carver, J. 2006. *Boards that make a difference: A new design for leadership in nonprofit and public organizations.* 3rd edition. San Francisco, CA: Jossey-Bass.

Charan, R., S. Drotter, and J. Noel. 2001. *The leadership pipeline: How to build the leadership-powered company.* San Francisco: Jossey-Bass.

Collins, J. 2001. *Good to great and the social sectors: why business thinking is not the answer: a monograph to accompany Good to great: why some companies make the leap . . . and others don't.* New York: Harper Business.

Collins, J. 2001. *Good to great: Why some companies make the leap—and others don't.* New York: Harper Business.

Ferriss, T. 2007. *The 4-hour work week: Escape 9-5, live anywhere, and join the new rich.* New York: Crown.

Heath, D. and C. Heath. 2007. *Made to stick: Why some ideas survive and others die.* New York: Random House.

Koch, R. 1997. *The 80/20 principle: The secret to success by achieving more with less.* New York: Doubleday Business.

Peters, T. 2004. *In search of excellence: lessons from America's best-run companies.* New York: Harper Business Essentials.

Reeves, D. 2004. *The 90/90/90 schools: a case study.* Chap. 19 in *Accountability in action: a blueprint for learning organizations.* Englewood, CO: Advanced Learning Press.

Thernstrom, A. 2003. *No excuses: closing the racial gap in learning.* New York: Simon & Schuster.

Trimble, J. R. 1975. *Writing with style: conversations on the art of writing.* Englewood Cliffs, NJ: Prentice-Hall.

About the Author

BRIAN CARPENTER is a crusader for excellence in charter school governance. His first book, *Charter School Board University*, has been read by thousands of board members and his monograph, *The Five Dysfunctions of Charter School Boards,* was included in Harvard University's summer seminar. A frequently sought after speaker and consultant, Dr. Carpenter distills 20 years of experience working for boards, with boards, and on boards into insightful, practical, and often-humorous lessons to help boards and executives work together more effectively.

You can network with Brian at www.LinkedIn.com.

Looking for Additional Resources?

To receive a group discount when ordering five or more copies of *The Seven Outs,* contact the National Charter Schools Institute at books@nationalcharterschools.org or call (989) 774-2999.

Looking for board orientation or board retreat materials? Brian's book, *Charter School Board University,* is now in its second edition. This unique primer on charter school governance is used by boards, authorizers and sponsors, state associations, and consultants across the country. To order, go to www.nationalcharterschools.org or call (989) 774-2999.

Are you interested in having Brian or another charter school expert from the National Charter Schools Institute speak at your event or consult with your organization? For information, contact the Institute at speaker@nationalcharterschools.org or call (989) 774-2999.

Did this book spark a question you would like Brian to answer? Receive a FREE personalized audio response from him. Email your question to resources@nationalcharterschools.org. Brian's answer, up to three minutes in duration, will be emailed to you as an MP3 audio file which you can play back on your computer and forward to your organizational colleagues.

Be sure to include your name, organization, and title in your email. Limit one question per person.